Great 2 x 4 Accessories for Your Home

Sterling Publishing Co., Inc. New York
A Sterling/Lark Book

Great 2 x 4 Accessories for Your Home

MAKING CANDLESTICKS, COATRACKS, MIRRORS, FOOTSTOOLS, AND MORE

Stevie Henderson and Mark Baldwin

In loving memory of

John Andrew Thompson
18 December 1914–25 January 1999

10 9 8 7 6 5 4 3 2

Published in 2002 by Lark Books, a division of
Sterling Publishing Company, Inc.
387 Park Avenue South, New York, NY 10016
©1999 by Stevie Henderson and Mark Baldwin
Distributed in Canada by Sterling Publishing
c/o Canadian Manda Group, One Atlantic Avenue, Suite 105
Toronto, Ontario, Canada M6K 3E7
Distributed in Great Britain by Chrysalis Books
64 Brewery Road, London N7 9NT, England
Distributed in Australia by Capricorn Link (Australia) Pty. Ltd.
P.O. Box 704, Windsor, NSW 2756, Australia

Printed in Hong Kong

Sterling ISBN 0-8069-9105-4

CONTENTS

INTRODUCTION 8

MATERIALS 9

TOOLS 16

TECHNIQUES 21

SAFETY 26

THE PROJECTS 27

Living Room and Hallway

WALL TABLE 29

OTTOMAN 32

COATRACK 37

SHELL MIRROR 40

GRANDMOTHER CLOCK 44

COFFEE TABLE 51

WALL LEDGE 55

Bedroom and Bath

CEDAR KEEPSAKE BOX 58

FOOTSTOOL 61

WASTEBASKET 64

WOODEN WINDOW VALANCE 68

FAUX POSTER BED 71

BIRDHOUSE FLOOR LAMP 78

BREAKFAST TRAY 82

Kitchen and Dining

KITCHEN ISLAND TOPPER 85

WINE CABINET 90

SCRAP-WOOD CANDLESTICKS 97

PLATE RACK 101

Home Office and Accessories

BIRDCAGE 105

DISPLAY BOX 111

FOLDING SCREEN 115

CD CABINET 119

DESK ORGANIZER 122

METRIC CONVERSION CHART 126

INDEX 127

INTRODUCTION

Everyone has to have basic furniture—a bed, a table, and somewhere to sit. But the space becomes your own when you add an ottoman, a folding screen, a wooden valance, or a grandmother clock. The accessory pieces in this book are not essential to furnishing a home, but we're willing to bet you'll find something in this book that you just have to have!

This was a particularly enjoyable book to put together, because the projects are just plain fun. Our previous books have contained "bread and butter" projects—basic furniture that everyone needs. This collection contains what we call "icing on the cake" projects—pieces that add flair and style to your home and make it unique and inviting.

All of the projects in this book are designed for beginners. If you can picture yourself cutting a board to length and nailing it to another board, you can make these projects. We hope that you will find just the right project to add that extra dash of style to your home.

MATERIALS

LUMBER

Regardless of your skill level or the complexity of the chosen project, it's a good idea to have some basic knowledge about the characteristics of various types of wood and which woods are most suitable for the chosen project. Different wood types have different grain patterns, fiber density, odors, and appearances. On the most basic level, all woods are classified as either *hardwood* or *softwood*. Softwood is cut from coniferous trees (or evergreens), such as pine, redwood, and cedar. Softwood is a good choice for the projects in this book—projects designed for the beginning woodworker—as it is easier to cut, drill, and nail than hardwood and has the added advantage of being much less expensive.

Hardwood, on the other hand, comes from deciduous trees (trees that shed their leaves annually), such as maple, cherry, and walnut. Though we have constructed the projects in this book from white pine, a readily available softwood, you can certainly use any hardwood of your choice (see page 11 for more information on substituting hardwood).

For purposes of clarity, this book refers to each surface of a board by a specific name. The broadest part of a board is called a *face*; the narrow surface along the length of the board is an *edge*; and the smallest surfaces on the extremities of each board are the *ends*.

Buying Lumber

Softwood is sold in standard dimensional sizes (2×4, 1×4, and 1×12, for example), and in specific lengths (6, 8, and 10 feet are common lengths). When you are searching for specific sizes in your local hardware store, a bin labeled 2×4×6 contains 2×4 s that are 6 feet in length.

A word about dimensions: Although it might appear that a 2×4 should be 2 inches thick and 4 inches wide, this is not the case. In fact, the term 2×4 describes the dimensions of the piece before it was planed to a smooth surface on all four sides. There is some method to the madness, however, and you can take comfort in knowing that all stock lumber is planed to the same dimensions—a 2×4 is (or very close to) $1\frac{1}{2}$ inches thick and $3\frac{1}{2}$ inches wide. See below for a chart that lists nominal sizes and actual sizes for softwood stock lumber.

Nominal Size	Actual Size
1×2	$\frac{3}{4}$" × $1\frac{1}{2}$"
1×3	$\frac{3}{4}$" × $2\frac{1}{2}$"
1×4	$\frac{3}{4}$" × $3\frac{1}{2}$"
1×6	$\frac{3}{4}$" × $5\frac{1}{2}$"
1×8	$\frac{3}{4}$" × $7\frac{1}{4}$"
1×10	$\frac{3}{4}$" × $9\frac{1}{4}$"
1×12	$\frac{3}{4}$" × $11\frac{1}{4}$"
2×2	$1\frac{1}{2}$" × $1\frac{1}{2}$"
2×4	$1\frac{1}{2}$" × $3\frac{1}{2}$"
2×6	$1\frac{1}{2}$" × $5\frac{1}{2}$"
2×8	$1\frac{1}{2}$" × $7\frac{1}{4}$"
2×10	$1\frac{1}{2}$" × $9\frac{1}{4}$"
2×12	$1\frac{1}{2}$" × $11\frac{1}{4}$"
4×4	$3\frac{1}{2}$" × $3\frac{1}{2}$"
4×6	$3\frac{1}{2}$" × $5\frac{1}{2}$"
6×6	$5\frac{1}{2}$" × $5\frac{1}{2}$"
8×8	$7\frac{1}{2}$" × $7\frac{1}{2}$"

Softwood is graded according to its quality. The higher the quality, the higher the price. Though it may be tempting to buy the highest quality wood, keep in mind that small imperfections can be covered with paint. Don't buy better quality than you need for the specific project. Softwood grades are as follows:

Common Grades

No. 1 COMMON contains knots and few imperfections, but should have no knotholes.

No. 2 COMMON is free of knotholes, but contains some knots.

No. 3 COMMON contains larger knots and small knotholes.

No. 4 COMMON is used for construction only. It contains large knotholes.

No. 5 COMMON is the lowest grade of lumber; it is used only when strength and appearance aren't important.

Select Grades

B AND BETTER (OR 1 AND 2 CLEAR) are the best and most expensive grades used for the finest furniture projects.

C SELECT may have a few small blemishes.

D SELECT is the lowest quality of the better board grades; it has imperfections that can be concealed with paint.

Select wood is higher quality than common wood and is more expensive. Clear boards come from the inner section of the tree, or the heartwood, and are nearly free of imperfections. Sapwood, or the outer portions of the tree, yields boards with more knots and other flaws.

Please read through the instructions and cutting list for your project before shopping for materials. Each materials list specifies the total number of linear feet of particular wood required to make the project. So if the total linear feet required is 40 feet, you can purchase five 8-foot lengths, four 10-foot lengths, and so on. When you arrive at the lumberyard or store, you may find that the 8-foot lengths of wood are of lesser quality than the 6-foot lengths. You could then buy seven 6-foot lengths and have a little left over, but you must first check to make certain that no single piece required by the project is over 6 feet long.

It is also wise to keep transportation abilities in mind. If you own (or can borrow) a pickup truck to transport your materials, board lengths are not a factor. But it's pretty difficult to get a 12-foot length of wood into a small car. Most building-supply stores will be happy to give you one free cut on an individual piece of lumber; some charge a fee.

Unless you have chosen a very expensive wood with which to build your project, it makes sense to slightly overbuy your materials. That way, if you do make a mistake, you have a reserve board to bail you out. Returning to the store for just one more board is frustrating, time consuming, and (depending upon how far you drive) sometimes more expensive than if you had purchased an extra board in the first place. We have built some overage into the materials list to accommodate squaring the piece and allowing for the width of saw cuts.

Selecting Lumber

Before purchasing any stock lumber, inspect each board for any defects and imperfections. It makes the trip to the lumber store more time consuming, but saves hours of frustration later. If the building-supply store will not allow you

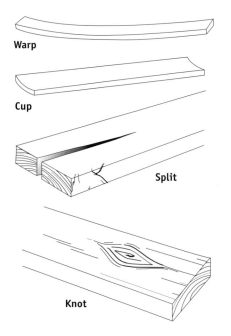

Warp

Cup

Split

Knot

to hand-pick individual boards, consider purchasing the lumber elsewhere. Some defects in wood can be corrected, but such corrections are time consuming — and choosing the wood carefully in the first place is the best way to get blemish-free boards. There is no reason to buy unusable wood, regardless of how low the price.

If you plan to paint the wood, small knots or blemishes are acceptable. (Bear in mind also that small knots on the ends of boards can sometimes be cut off; be sure to purchase a large enough board to allow for the waste.) Large knotholes should be avoided; there is always the chance that they will fall out and leave a large hole behind.

Since some building-supply stores purchase wood from many different suppliers, the board widths may vary slightly between boards. Although this may seem to be a minor point, know that even $1/64$ of an inch difference may mean that pieces will not fit together properly.

To make sure the boards are all the same length, simply position the boards on top of each other to make certain they are all exactly the same.

Another common problem with stock lumber is that it has a tendency to warp and bow. Though it is possible to straighten warped wood, purchasing straight wood is much easier. To check for warping or bowing, place one end of the board on the floor and look down the length of its face. Next, turn the board and look down its edge. By examining the board in this way, any warps or bows will be obvious.

Avoid split boards; check the ends as well as the rest of the board. Split boards do tend to separate lengthwise into two (unusable) boards. Again, it is possible to cut off end splits, but be sure you purchase enough wood to allow for the waste.

Substituting Hardwood

Any of the projects in the book can be built with hardwood, though you'll need to make some extra calculations to do so. Hardwood will resist scratches and dents much better than softwood, but it is more difficult to work with and significantly more expensive.

Because it is cut from logs as wide and as long as possible, hardwood is normally sold in random widths and lengths. Consequently, hardwood is sold by a measure called the *board foot*, which represents a piece of lumber 1 inch thick (or less), 12 inches wide, and 1 foot long. Board foot measurements usually indicate that the lumber is rough, not surfaced.

Hardwood thicknesses are measured in quarter inches; the standard thicknesses are 4/4, 5/4, 6/4, and 8/4 (pronounced "four-quarter," "five-quarter," and so forth, not "four-fourths").

To calculate board feet, multiply the thickness by the width in inches, then multiply the length in feet and divide by 12. A 4/4 oak plank 6 inches wide and 10 feet long is 5 board feet (BF). The board-foot measurement is doubled for boards thicker than 1 inch. **Note:** Even if the boards you buy have been thickness-planed to ¾ inch, you pay for 4/4 lumber.

Plywood

As you might expect, plywood is made from several plies, or layers, of wood that are glued together. You can find two principal kinds of plywood: veneer-core and lumber-core. Because they are unattractive, the edges of veneer-core plywood must be either filled or covered. Lumber-core plywood is higher in quality, and the edges can be worked just as you would any solid wood.

Plywood is usually sold in sheets measuring 4 feet by 8 feet, though in some building-supply stores, it is available in half-sheets measuring 4 feet by 4 feet. A variety of thicknesses are available; the standard thicknesses are ⅛, ¼, ⅜, ½, ⅝, and ¾ inch.

Another indicator of plywood quality is the grade of its outer veneer. You will find plywood in grades A through D, with A representing the best quality. In addition, each piece of plywood has two grades, one for each face. Thus, an A–C piece has one surface that is A quality and one that is C. Check also to see if plywood is designated exterior or interior. Exterior-grade has waterproof glue between the plies; do not use interior-grade plywood for outside projects, as it will warp and split when exposed to the elements for even a short period of time.

FINISHES

Paint

One of the biggest advantages of painting your project is that paint will cover or camouflage most flaws in the wood. You will be surprised at how fabulous a not-so-attractive piece will look once you've applied a coat of high-quality paint. The downside is that wood needs to be thoroughly filled, sanded, and primed before you paint—which takes time and effort. If you plan to paint your project, you can buy a lower grade of wood.

Purchase high-quality paint—it pays off, since it looks much better and often requires less paint. When shopping for paint, look for special characteristics that protect against local weather problems. For example, here in Florida, many paints protect against mildew, which occurs in areas with high humidity. (The paint store can sometimes add a mildew-resistant substance to regular paint.) Also, look to see how long the paint is warranted.

Stain

If you plan to stain your project, you will need to make this decision before you purchase the

FINISHING MATERIALS Clockwise from left: wood filler and putty knife, assortment of finishes and stains, disposable foam brushes, and a natural-bristle brush

wood. Buy boards that have few imperfections and similar grain patterns.

Stains have come a long way. They used to come only in shades of brown and be very difficult to apply evenly. These days, stains are available in a terrific variety of colors, from the palest white to the darkest black. They can be extremely translucent or nearly opaque. And best of all, most stains are now quite easy to apply, usually requiring only one coat.

Although most manufacturers suggest applying stain with a brush, we have found that a clean rag provides a very smooth, even appearance. The degree of success using this technique varies among different types of stains, so make sure you test first on a scrap piece of wood or on a surface of your project that will not show before you begin. Before using any product, read the instructions carefully and follow them explicitly.

BRUSHES

Though some experts swear by expensive paint-brushes, we use foam brushes almost exclusively, since they are extremely cheap and can be thrown away after each use. This helps with cleanup and makes the entire process more simple. Look for the ones that have a smooth surface (like a cosmetic sponge) and a wooden handle. Don't buy the ones that look like kitchen sponges with visible holes on their surfaces.

A tip: If you need to interrupt the job temporarily, simply insert the brush into an airtight plastic sandwich bag. You can leave it there for several days, and it will remain pliable and ready to use.

ADHESIVES

Aliphatic resin, which is commonly marketed as wood glue or carpenter's glue, is the most widely used woodworking adhesive. The main consideration when using wood glue is quantity. Do not overdo it. If too much glue is used, the glue will squeeze out of the joint and drip onto your project when pressure is applied.

Apply a small ribbon of glue down the center of one surface then rub the adjoining surface against the ribbon to distribute the glue evenly. Coat both surfaces with a uniform, thin coating. Wipe off drips quickly with a damp cloth. If drips are allowed to dry on the surface of the wood, they will harden and require sanding to remove. Do not leave glue drips; they will not accept most stains and will always show up as a different color, even under a clear finish.

FASTENERS

Nails

The list of nail varieties is long: common, large flathead, duplex head, and oval head are just a sampling. The type most commonly used in woodworking is the finish nail. Finish nails have a much smaller head than the common nail, making them easy to recess below the surface of the wood, or countersink. When a finish nail is countersunk, the small hole remaining on the surface of the wood is easily concealed with wood filler.

Nail sizes are designated by "penny" (abbreviated as "d"). A nail's penny size corresponds directly to its length, although the nail diameter is larger for longer nails. Finish nails range in length from 1 inch to 6 inches. An easy way to determine the penny size of a nail up to 3 inches

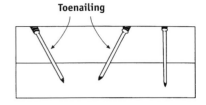

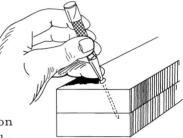

An assortment of screws (top), nails (left), and brads (right)

(10d): take the length of the nail you need, subtract ½ inch, and multiply by 4. For example, if you need a 2½-inch nail, subtract ½ inch, leaving 2. Next, multiply by 4. What you need is an 8-penny nail (8d). Refer to the table below for commonly used nail sizes:

Penny Size	Length (in inches)
2d	1
3d	1¼
4d	1½
5d	1¾
6d	2
7d	2¼
8d	2½
9d	2¾
10d	3
12d	3¼
16d	3½
20d	4

A good general rule to follow when choosing a nail is to use a nail that will provide the greatest amount of holding power without penetrating the opposite surface. For example, if you are joining two 1×4s, each piece of wood is ¾ inch thick—a total of 1½ inches of wood. For such a project, you should choose a 1¼-inch (3d) nail.

Keep in mind that nails driven at an angle provide more holding power than those driven straight into the wood. The term *toenailing* refers to the method of driving a nail into wood at an extreme angle to secure two pieces together. The most difficult part of toenailing comes when the nail is nearly into the wood and only the head and a bit of the shank are visible.

To avoid making hammer marks on the wood, hammer the nail into the piece until the head is still slightly above the surface. Then use a nail set to finish the job and countersink the nail (see illustration, right). Indeed, the best way to avoid leaving hammer marks on the wood is to use a nail set. The trick to using a nail set effectively is holding it in the proper manner. The set should be steadied with the hand by gripping it firmly with all four fingers and the thumb. Rest the little finger on the surface of the wood for added stability.

It is a good idea to predrill nail holes, especially if you are working with hardwood, a very narrow piece of softwood, or any other wood that has a tendency to split. Use a drill bit that is just barely smaller than the diameter of the nail, and drill a pilot hole about two-thirds the diameter of the nail.

Brads

Wire brads, which are a thinner and smaller version of finish nails, are extremely useful for attaching trim and molding, as well as for very small projects. They are designated in length in inches and wire gauge numbers from 11 to 20. The lower the gauge number, the larger the diameter.

Toenailing

Screws

Screws have more holding power than nails and have the additional advantage of being easily removed (when used without glue) at a later date. However, screws are more difficult to insert.

There are many kinds of screws. In woodworking, flathead Phillips screws are the most commonly used. This type of screw has a flat head that can be countersunk. It is most often labeled as a "drywall screw" and can be driven with a power drill.

Screws are designated by length and diameter. As with nails, you want to use the longest screw possible that won't penetrate the opposite surface. Screw diameter is designated by gauge numbers, with the most common gauge numbers ranging from #2 to #16. Larger diameters have higher gauge numbers. The projects in this book use screws with gauge numbers from #6 to #10.

Do not be stingy with screws; that being said, you do not want to insert so many screws into your project that the metal outweighs the wood. If there is any chance that the joint is not secure, add extra screws. Your project, after all, may need to hold up to several moves over the course of the years, which will place additional strain on the joints.

It is possible to countersink a screw in very soft wood simply by driving it with a power drill. However, the resulting surface hole must be covered, either with wood filler or by predrilling the screw hole and inserting a wood plug on top of the countersunk screw head.

Predrilling is normally a two-step operation. First drill the larger, countersunk portion at a diameter just larger than the diameter of the

screw head and deep enough to accommodate it. If a wood plug is to be used, use a bit with the same diameter as the plug. Next, drill the pilot hole in the center of the larger hole, using a drill bit the same diameter as the solid portion of the screw (minus the threads). If you use the same size screws on a regular basis, you may wish to invest in a combination pilot/countersink bit for your drill, which will perform both functions at the same time.

Wood plugs can be purchased, or you can cut your own by slicing a wooden dowel. The only disadvantage to plugs you make is that the plug will show the end grain and will be visible if the wood is stained. An alternative is to cut wood plugs using a plug cutter, but that method requires a drill press.

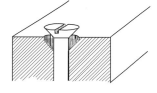

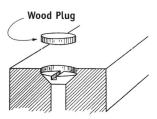

Wood Plug

Screws can be inserted at an angle, the same way that nails are, to toenail two pieces of wood together (see page 14). It takes a little practice, but inserting a screw at an angle gets easier. A drill or a screw starter makes this process easier by beginning the screw hole.

Staple Guns and Staples

Staples are light-duty fasteners that are often used to attach fabric to wood. It is a good idea to invest in a staple gun—it's a useful tool to have around the house for a variety of jobs. They are available in a variety of sizes, styles, and price ranges. Electric staple guns are handy, to be sure, but a simple, heavy-duty gun is a good beginning. Purchase staples in a variety of lengths to accommodate different thicknesses of wood.

TOOLS

WORK SURFACE

A smooth and level work surface is essential in woodworking. It is nearly impossible to get table legs perfectly even on an uneven surface. Your work surface does not have to be elaborate or professional-quality (or even attractive)—it just has to be level and even. It can be as simple as an old, unpaneled door or a piece of thick plywood.

To make sure your work surface is level, simply set a long level in various spots on the surface, turning it so that it faces several directions. In addition, stand back and sight along the surface to make sure it isn't twisted. If you need to lift the surface to make it perfectly level, attach a shim with glue and nails or screws.

MEASURING TOOLS

MEASURING TOOLS Clockwise from top right: combination square, adjustable bevel, carpenter's square, measuring tape, conventional level, straightedge, and electronic level

An **adjustable bevel** is a useful measuring tool; it helps establish bevel angles, and checks and transfers bevels and mitered ends. It has a steel blade that pivots and slides within a handle, and can be locked into position to form an angle.

Squares are important tools in woodworking, as they make it easier to mark an accurate cutting line and to obtain a right angle. They are also useful for performing many additional functions, such as checking the outer or inner squareness of a joint and guiding a saw through a cut. The most commonly used types are the combination square and the framing square (or carpenter's square).

A **straightedge**, or a steel ruler 12 to 24 inches long, is a great tool to have on hand for quick measurements.

A **wide steel tape rule** works much better than a narrow tape, because its rigidity allows for more accurate cuts. (A narrow tape will bend more easily along the length of the board.)

CUTTING TOOLS

CUTTING TOOLS Clockwise from top: squaring jig, jigsaw, miter box and saw, backsaw, coping saw and blades, carpenter's handsaw, and circular saw

LEFT: router and bits. **RIGHT:** battery-operated power drill with drill bits

An assortment of screwdrivers

An assortment of nail sets (left) and hammers (right)

A **circular saw** has a blade that can be adjusted to cut a 90° angle, a 45° angle, or any angle in between. It is probably the most popular power cutting tool.

A **crosscut saw** is made for crosscutting, or cutting across the width (and the grain) of the wood. They are available with 7 through 12 points per inch, depending on how coarse or fine you wish the cut to be. The greater the number, the smoother (and slower) the cut.

A **rip saw** has teeth designed for ripping, or cutting along the length of the board (with the grain). It comes with 4½ though 7 points per inch, the latter being the smoothest cut.

Although there are **saw blades** designed specifically for ripping and crosscutting, the most practical blade for general woodworking projects (such as the ones in this book) is the combination blade, which rips and crosscuts with equal ease. Carbide-tipped blades are more expensive, but well worth the cost, since they last much longer than regular blades.

The hand-held **jigsaw**, or **saber saw**, is used to cut curves, shapes, and large hole in panels or boards up to 1½ inches in thickness. Its cutting action comes from a narrow reciprocating "bayo-net" blade that moves up and down very quickly. The most useful jigsaws have a variable speed control and an orbital blade action, which swings the cutting edge forward into the work and back again during the blade's up-and-down cycle—and a dust blower that keeps the sawdust away from the cut.

A **power miter saw** is one of our favorite tools. It can be used to efficiently cut boards to length and can be adjusted both horizontally and vertically from 0° to 45°. It is especially useful for cutting 45° miters, though an inexpensive miter box and saw also work for this purpose.

An assortment of chisels and a plane (center)

Chisels are useful for performing unique wood-working tasks, such as hollowing out a small section of wood. Using chisels takes some practice, but is worth the effort. Make sure your chisels are sharp and that you have at least two: one very narrow one and one about ½ inch wide.

A **plane** is useful for shaving a small section of wood from the end or the edge of a board when the need arises. Buy a high-quality plane and keep it very sharp. Practice with it until you feel comfortable with the cutting technique.

CLAMPS

You will need a variety of clamps to make the projects in this book. Clamps are valuable tools in assembling projects, because they apply pressure and hold joints together until the glue sets. Clamps are generally used in pairs, so always buy two of any particular style of clamp.

Clamps make working alone much easier, since they allow a single person to assemble a large project. A new type of clamp is now available that can be operated with one hand. This type, which comes in a variety of lengths, looks similar to a regular bar clamp (see below), but instead of tightening it by turning a screw mechanism, you squeeze its double handle as you would that of a caulk gun. They are easy to use, work well, and have a quick-release mechanism.

When working with clamps, always insert a scrap piece of wood between the clamp and your work to act as a cushion, especially when working with softwoods. This technique prevents clamp marks on the surface of the wood.

Old-fashioned **wood clamps** are great, since they can be adjusted to clamp offsetting surfaces. You should have several around your workshop to use for this purpose.

CLAMPS Clockwise from top: wood clamps, light-duty bar clamps, spring clamps, pipe clamp, and C clamp (center)

Spring clamps are useful when you need to quickly hold a piece of wood while you saw or keep two thin boards positioned. The 2-inch size is most useful because you can operate it with one hand.

Bar clamps and **pipe clamps** are useful for holding assemblies together temporarily while you add the fastener. They can also be used to apply pressure to laminates. Bar clamps and pipe clamps look very similar and function in essentially the same way, though pipe clamps are significantly less expensive. The fittings for pipe clamps are sold separately—and they can be used for various lengths of pipe. You can also purchase rubber "shoes" that fit over the pipe-clamp fittings, which will prevent clamp marks on wood. Remember to put pieces of plastic or wax paper between the pipes and any glue lines they come in contact with, because a chemical reaction between the glue and the pipe can leave a dark stain on the surface of the wood.

Web clamps, also called **band clamps**, are used for clamping such things as chairs or drawers, where a uniform pressure needs to be exerted completely around a project. They consist of a continuous band with an attached metal mechanism that can be ratcheted to pull the band tightly around the object.

C Clamps are inexpensive and quite useful for a number of woodworking tasks. They can hold two thicknesses of wood together, secure a piece of wood to a work surface, and perform many other functions. One end of the C-shaped frame is fixed, and the other end is fitted with a threaded rod and swivel pad that can be clamped tightly across an opening ranging from zero to several inches or more, depending on the size of the clamp.

SANDING TOOLS Clockwise from top right: orbital sander, finishing sander, an assortment of sandpaper, sanding block (center), and belt sander

SANDING TOOLS

There are a variety of options for sanding projects. Of course, any wood surface can be sanded by hand, though hand-sanding may prove time consuming. For sanding by hand, any inexpensive plastic sanding block will work just fine on a level surface. An even more inexpensive version is to wrap a block of wood with a piece of sandpaper. For sanding moldings, curves, or any other small spaces, wrap a pencil or other appropriately sized object with sandpaper.

The amount of sanding required for any given project depends on, to a large degree, the intended use of the project and the kind of finish you plan to use. If you prefer a rustic look, the project need not be sanded completely smooth. (However, a rustic chair requires more sanding than a rustic table, since someone will be sitting on it.)

An **orbital sander** is useful for beginning the sanding process, but it may leave circular marks that must be sanded out by hand.

A **finishing sander** is probably the most practical power sander for furniture projects. It can smooth the surface of the wood very quickly, and it does not leave circular marks.

For large jobs, a **belt sander** may be the best choice. It sands quickly, but it is difficult to control on softwood, such as pine. Because of its power, a belt sander can easily gouge softwood or, if you don't watch carefully, it can remove more of the wood than you wish.

Regardless of the sanding tool you choose, begin sanding with coarse grit and gradually progress to sandpaper with a fine grit. An open-coat aluminum oxide paper is best for sanding both softwoods and hardwoods. Throw sandpaper away as soon as it quits working; there's no sense prolonging the job to save a few cents.

Tools Checklist

THE ESSENTIALS

Work surface that is smooth and level

Measuring tools: tape measure, level, and combination square

Hammers and nails: large hammer, small hammer, tack hammer, and nail set

Screwdrivers (hand and/or power): assortment of flathead and Phillips sizes

Saws: combination saw (or ripsaw and crosscut saw), circular saw, and a selection of blades

Drill: hand or power drill and a variety of bits

Clamps: two "quick clamps," two wood hand clamps, and a few 2-inch spring clamps

Sanding tools: sanding block and an assortment of sandpaper (from fine to coarse)

OPTIONAL TOOLS

Measuring tools: framing square

Saws: saber saw, circular saw, and a selection of blades

Chisels: ¼-inch, ¾-inch, and 1-inch wide

Finishing sander

Router

Safety equipment: goggles and dust mask (for use with power tools)

Miter box

Woodworking vise or portable vise/work table

Clamps: two C clamps, a web clamp, two light-duty bar clamps, and two pipe clamps

ADVANCED TOOLS

Belt sander

Table saw

Band saw

Drill press

TECHNIQUES

MEASURING LUMBER

Nothing is more frustrating than gathering the necessary materials and embarking upon a project only to find that inaccurate cutting has made it impossible for the pieces to fit together properly—and thus for the project to look right. Woodworking projects, regardless of the skill level, go much more smoothly if you follow the old adage "measure twice—cut once."

The best way to make good cuts is to measure accurately. There are a number of tools that will help with this: a wide steel tape rule, a square, and a variety of saws (see page 16 for more information on choosing tools). It is essential that you buy or borrow quality tools. Whatever tools you choose, use the same measuring device throughout the project, as two instruments may vary enough to make a difference.

CUTTING LUMBER

The most important rule of thumb in cutting lumber is to cut the longest piece first. If you botch the cut, then you can still cut smaller pieces from the remaining board. It is also important to re-examine each piece of lumber one last time before you cut; this is useful in spotting end splits or knots that can be cut off.

If you plan carefully, you can cut so that all the best sides of the wood are facing out—this makes for the best possible use of your wood, and saves you from having to fill and sand any imperfections after the project is finished.

Every time you use a blade to cut wood, the blade removes an amount of wood equal to the width of its saw blade, called the *kerf*. After you have precisely measured for a cut and marked it with a sharp pencil, set the saw so that the blade will exactly remove the waste side of the mark. Cut along the mark, trying to remove just half of your pencil line.

There are two types of cuts that can be made to a piece of wood: a rip or a crosscut. A rip is a cut along the length of the board, and a crosscut is a cut across the width of the board. There are specific hand tools for each procedure; see page 16 for detailed information on these cutting tools.

When you are cutting either lumber or plywood, note the type of cut that your tool is making, and use it to your advantage. For example, circular saws and jigsaws cut on the upstroke, so they may leave ragged edges on the upper surface of the wood. When using these saws, you should position the wood with the better surface facing down when cutting.

There is an accurate method for cutting a length of wood to fit between two existing pieces in an assembly. After you square off the wood you are cutting, simply hold it up to the actual space, and mark it for cutting.

MAKING WOOD JOINTS

Though there are hundreds of different kinds of wood joints—from plain butt joints to incredibly intricate and complex joints—the projects in this book are constructed with only the simplest joints, secured with glue and either nails or screws. No matter what kind of joint you're making, it is advisable to use both glue and fasteners (nails or screws) whenever possible. The only exception, when you may want to omit the glue, is on joints that you wish to disassemble at a later date.

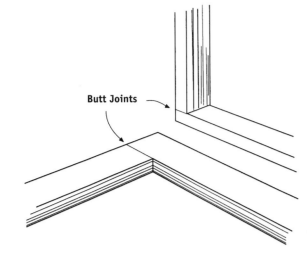

Butt Joints

Butt Joints

The simplest of joints, butt joints are formed when one board abuts another at a right angle. Though butt joints are easy, they offer the least amount of holding power of any joint and must be reinforced with a fastener, usually screws.

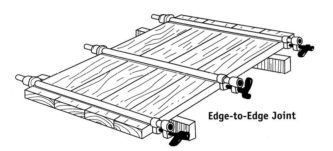

Edge-to-Edge Joint

Edge-to-Edge Joint

Edge-to-edge joints are used when laminating boards together edge to edge to obtain a wider piece of wood. To create an edge-to-edge joint, a minuscule amount of wood should be ripped from the first edge of each board in order to ensure a perfect meeting between boards. The boards should be flipped widthwise and the second edge ripped.

Once the edges of the boards have been ripped, apply glue to the adjoining edges and clamp the boards together. Apply even clamping pressure along the length of the piece. Wipe off any excess glue that is squeezed out in the clamping

process. The boards should be firmly clamped, but not so tightly that all of the glue is forced out or that the lamination starts to bow across its width. On a long lamination, extra boards may be placed across the width above and below the lamination. The extra boards are then clamped with C clamps or wood clamps. (It is a good idea to place a piece of plastic or wax paper between the work piece and any wood clamped across the joints; this will prevent the clamped board from becoming a permanent part of the finished lamination.)

Dado

A dado is a groove cut in the face of one board to accommodate the thickness of another board. It can be cut with a handsaw and a chisel (see below), with a router, or with a dado set on a table saw.

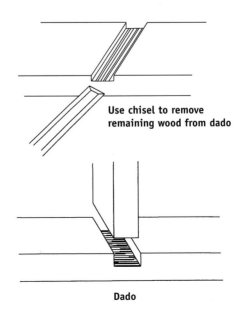

Cut dado to depth with saw

Use chisel to remove remaining wood from dado

Dado

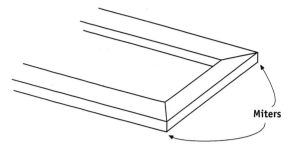

Miters

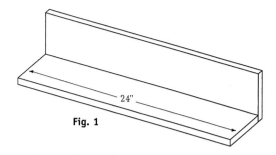

Miter

A miter is an angle cut across the width of a board. It is used to join the ends of two pieces of wood at an angle without exposing the end grain of either piece. A mitered joint must also be reinforced with nails or screws and is most often cut to 45°. Two boards mitered to 45° angles are then used to construct a right angle.

The most important consideration when making miters is careful measurement. When cutting and applying molding, begin at one end, cut the first piece and attach it. Then cut the first angle on the second piece, hold it in place, and mark the cut (and the direction of that cut) on the other end. Since you are usually switching directions of 45° angles on each successive cut, this method avoids confusion. Attach the second piece, and continue the process for each subsequent piece. A helpful tip to make your miter joints look more perfect than they are: Firmly rub the length of the completed joint with the side of a pencil to smooth the two edges together.

Miters on Crown Moldings

Crown moldings, which have curves on one face and two bevels on the other, can be tricky to miter. We have come up with a simple, shop-made jig to make this process much easier. To make the fabulous Crown Molding Mitering Jig, follow these steps:

1. Cut two bases from 1×6 pine, each measuring 24 inches long.

2. Place one base on a level surface, as shown in figure 1.

3. Place the second base on edge against one edge of the first base, as shown in figure 1. Apply glue to the meeting surfaces and screw through the second base into the edge of the first base. Use 1⅝-inch screws spaced about every 4 inches.

4. Label the first base "bottom." Label the second base "top." These labels do not necessarily indicate the top and bottom of the molding to be cut, as that will depend on where the molding will be installed. We'll use the labels for the rest of the construction steps.

5. Use a combination square to mark a 45° angle on the top surface of the bottom of the guide. Square a line up the face of the top from the end of the angled line. Finally, mark another 45° angle on the edge of the top of the guide, starting at the vertical line, as shown in figure 2.

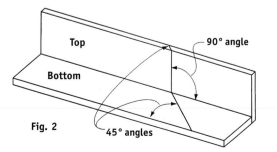

6. Use a backsaw to cut through the top and into (but not through) the bottom.

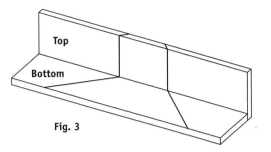

Fig. 3

7. Repeat steps 5 and 6 to mark and cut a mirror-image 45° angle, as shown in figure 3.

To Cut Crown Molding

1. Place the coved edge (the edge that will be on the "inside" of the miter) of the crown molding against the "top" of the guide, as shown in figure 4. Match your mark to the appropriate kerf in the top of the guide. Nail through the crown molding into the guide, using two small finish nails on the side of the molding. This will keep the molding from shifting during the cutting process. Depending on the molding you are mitering, spring clamps may work, too.

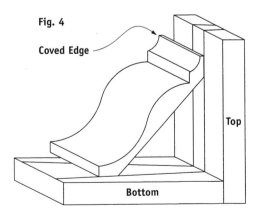

Fig. 4

Coved Edge

Top

Bottom

2. Follow the kerf in the guide to saw through the crown molding to produce a 45° miter.

Bevel

A bevel is also an angular cut; unlike a miter, it refers to an angle cut along the length of a board, rather than across the width.

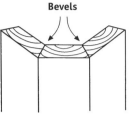

Bevels

DECORATIVE PAINTING

We used several decorative painting techniques to finish our projects. All of these techniques are easy to do, and require very few tools.

Sponge Painting

Sponge painting is a two-layer procedure. The first step is to paint the project a solid color. Then a second color is applied over the first with a sponge. We prefer to use a natural sea sponge because of its irregular shape. Wear rubber gloves, since the procedure is pretty messy. To sponge paint, just pour some paint into a paint tray, and dip the sponge into the paint. Remove the excess paint by pressing the sponge lightly on a newspaper or butcher paper. The idea is to sponge on a light painted texture, but not to end up with large blobs of paint. Continue the procedure over the entire surface, turning the sponge in a different direction each time so the texture is even, but not repetitive.

The wonderful thing about sponge painting is that if you don't like what you have done, you can simply repaint all or a portion of the project, then sponge again. If you want a very subtle look, choose two paints that are close to the same color (such as bright white and off-white). For a more dramatic look, choose contrasting colors, such as off-white and bright pink. Don't be afraid to experiment—you can always repaint. For a very subtle texture, try sponge painting two layers over the base color as we did for the Faux Poster Bed (page 71). Let the first sponged layer dry before sponging with the second color.

Glazing

Glazing is a semitransparent coat of paint that can be applied to either a solid color or over another painting technique (such as sponge painting). The glaze itself is transparent, but when mixed with another paint (the usual proportions are ¾ glaze and ¼ regular paint), it becomes a very subtle tint. We have used it over sponge painting to lessen the contrast between the first coat and the sponge paint, as on the Folding Screen (page 115).

To glaze, mix the glaze medium with paint following the manufacturer's directions. Then apply the glaze over the base coat with either a brush or roller.

Stamping

Stamping has become a very popular technique, and there are thousands of different stamps to choose from. It's incredibly easy to stamp. The only thing to remember is that the paint must be applied to the stamp with a brush, then stamped on the surface. Experiment by stamping the design onto butcher paper or newspaper to figure out how much paint should be applied to the stamp. If you dip the stamp directly into the paint, you will end up stamping blobs onto your surface.

If you don't reload your stamp with paint the second time you use it, the image will be lighter and will produce a different look. Using two

different colors of paint on the same stamp also gives an interesting contrast. Or try stamping with one color first, then clean your stamp and use the same stamp with a different color, as we did with the Folding Screen (page 115).

You can also create stamps by cutting up ordinary commercial sponges, as we did for the Wooden Valance (page 68). For that project, we cut a square out of a dishwashing sponge, then used the sponge to stamp.

SAFETY

Woodworking, particularly working with power tools, can be very dangerous. It is not uncommon for woodworkers to have missing digits. It pays to treat power tools with respect—and be a little scared of them. Keep a first-aid kit and a phone handy. Read the instructions that are provided with every tool and follow them religiously. The instructions in this book are written for the beginner using hand tools and must be altered when using power tools. Never attempt a maneuver that is not appropriate to the power tool you are using. Misuse of power tool equipment can lead to serious injury to yourself or damage to the tool.

When using power tools, it is essential to remember that you should never take your eyes off what you are doing. Always concentrate on

the work at hand, and take the necessary safety precautions as outlined in the tool's owner's manual. Just a moment of lost concentration or not following the safety rules can result in frightful consequences. Develop the habit of avoiding the path of the saw; do not stand directly behind it or directly in front of it. Power saws can flip a piece of wood back at you with incredible force.

Safety goggles or glasses should be worn at all times when working with wood. If you manage to avoid just one splinter aimed at your eye, you will be happy you bothered. Wearing a dust mask is also a good idea, since sawdust can be very irritating to your eyes and your lungs. There are several types of dust masks available, from a simple paper mask to those with replaceable filters.

Once you've taken steps to protect your digits, your eyes, and your lungs, invest in a pair of earplugs. Prolonged exposure to loud noise—like that from a circular saw, for example—can have harmful effects on your hearing.

One last plug for using protective gear: Safe practice in the workshop allows you to insulate yourself from the irritating aspects of woodworking, and to concentrate better on (and enjoy more fully) the work at hand.

SAFETY EQUIPMENT Clockwise from top left: ear protectors, commercial first-aid kit, safety goggles, safety glasses, and dust mask

THE PROJECTS

You're anxious to get started on your first project, to buy the lumber, then begin cutting and hammering and building something fabulous. Take just a few minutes more to read this section. We've included some basic information on how the instructions are organized—as well as a few tips that will save you time, money, and frustration.

MATERIALS

The list of materials for each project specifies in linear feet the amount of wood you will need. Where we have specified pine, we simply mean a decent grade of dimensional lumber. Feel free to use whatever lumber is more readily available in your area. We have allowed slight overage in the number of feet required, to square the ends of each board and to cover waste, but it is always prudent to overbuy slightly. A trip back to the store to buy another 2×4 is frustrating.

For purposes of clarity in the project instructions, each board surface has been named. The broadest board surface is called its face, and the narrow surface along the length is its edge. The ends, obviously, are the smallest surfaces at each end of the board.

HARDWARE

We have also specified the number of nails, screws, and other hardware you will need for the project you have chosen. We recognize that you will purchase nails and screws by the box, and will not actually buy "12 nails," but our total will give you a reference amount. Again, it is always prudent to have extra supplies on hand.

TOOLS AND TECHNIQUES

When applicable, we have provided a list of special tools that you may not have and techniques that you may need to learn. Check the list before you go shopping. If it calls for a staple gun and you don't own one, you need to decide whether to purchase (or borrow) a staple gun or select another project. If the project calls for dados and you aren't familiar with the term, read through that portion of the techniques section before you begin the project.

If you are an advanced woodworker who possesses large stationary power tools, it is particularly important to read through the project instructions before beginning, since you will probably want to modify the procedures to accommodate your advanced knowledge and tools. Bear in mind that these instructions are written for very basic tools, and some techniques may need to be "translated" in order to use your tools safely. For instance, a dado may be cut by hand, on a table saw, or with a router, but each of these methods requires a different setup and specific knowledge of the tools involved. Know the capabilities of your tools, and don't exceed them.

CUTTING LIST

We have provided an exact guide for cutting each piece of wood for your project. Don't cut all the pieces right away. The instructions will walk you through cutting each piece as it is required in the building process. Do, however, read through the cutting list before you shop for your materials. If your project calls for an 8-foot length, you shouldn't purchase all your 1×4s in 6-foot lengths.

Inspect each piece of wood before you buy it. Avoid buying wood that is warped, twisted, or cupped. The easiest way to check a board is to place one end on the floor and look down the length of its face. Then turn the board and look down its edge. Any unwanted curves will be obvious immediately. See page 9 for more information on inspecting and purchasing lumber.

Also keep in mind that you will have to transport the lumber home. If your project requires 10-foot lengths of wood, and you drive a small car, call a friend to borrow a pickup truck or have the wood delivered. It is also important to consider how you want to finish the surface of the project. Lower grades of wood can be used if you plan to paint, because wood filler and paint will cover many imperfections. If you plan to stain the wood, choose a better grade and pick boards with similar grain patterns.

A cutting hint: Cut the longest project pieces first. If you miscut, you'll still have plenty of wood to cut another piece. Pay some attention to the size of waste wood. Try to produce cutoffs that can be used for other pieces in the project.

BEFORE YOU BEGIN

Read and review all the instructions carefully, and visualize the process before you begin. The more you understand about the project you are going to make and how the process should proceed, the smoother the work will go. Woodworking is a step-by-step process, in which one step must be completed before the next one is begun. The slightest error in one step can drastically change the outcome of a project. If you understand where the next piece goes and cut it just before you use it, you can check to make sure that your assembly is truly accurate and adjust any small imperfections.

You will not avoid making mistakes in woodworking. The key is to learn from them. Consider woodworking to be a constantly evolving process. If you slip up several times in a row, take a break and come back to it. Your projects will turn out better, and you will be a safer and more satisfied woodworker.

Wall Table

This suspended table is a nice addition to a neglected area in an entryway. It takes up no floor space, is only about 9 inches deep, and makes a perfect surface for a small plant and a few odd decorative items.

MATERIALS

11 linear feet of 1×8 pine

5 linear feet of 1×4 pine

3 linear feet of 1×2 pine*

HARDWARE

35 1½" (4d) finish nails

12 1½" wood screws

CUTTING LIST

Code	Description	Qty.	Materials	Dimensions
A	Top/Bottom	2	1×8 pine	36" long
B	Front	1	1×8 pine	36" long
C	Sides	2	1×8 pine	7¼" long
D	Triangular Trim	8	1×4 pine	6¼"×4⅞"×4⅞"
E	Support	1	1×2 pine	30" long

Note on Materials: Because 1×2 pine will be used as the inner support for the table, you may substitute any scrap wood for this piece, as long as it is approximately 30 inches long.

CONSTRUCTING THE TABLE

1. Cut two Top/Bottoms (A) from 1×8 pine, each measuring 36 inches.

2. Cut one Front (B) from 1×8 pine, measuring 36 inches.

3. Place the Top/Bottoms (A) and the Front (B) on a level surface, parallel to each other and 5½ inches apart.

4. Apply glue to the top edges of the Top/Bottoms (A). Place the Front (B) over the top edges of the Top/Bottoms (A) as shown in figure 1. Nail through the Front (B) into the edges of the Top/Bottoms (A), using 1½-inch nails spaced 5 inches apart.

5. Cut two Sides (C) from 1×8 pine, each measuring 7¼ inches.

6. Apply glue to the meeting surfaces, and attach one Side (C) to one open end of the assembly as shown in figure 2. Nail through the Side (C) into the edges of the Top/Bottoms (A) and Front (B), using two 1½-inch nails on each joint.

7. Repeat step 6 to attach the remaining Side (C) to the other (open) end of the assembly.

ADDING THE TRIANGULAR TRIM

1. Cut eight Triangular Trims (D) from 1×8 pine, each measuring 6¼ × 4⅞ × 4⅞ inches.

2. Sand all edges of each of the Triangular Trims (D).

3. Place the table assembly front side up on a level surface. Place six evenly spaced Triangular Trims (D) across the Front (B), even with the top edge of the table, as shown in figure 3. After sanding, you will have minuscule spaces between the Triangular Trims (D).

4. Apply glue to the meeting surfaces, and attach the six Triangular Trims (D) to the Front (B) using two 1½-inch nails for each Trim (D). Nail through the Triangular Trims (D) into the Front (B).

5. Center one Triangular Trim (D) on the top edge of one Side (C).

6. Apply glue to the meeting surfaces, and attach the Triangular Trim (D) to the Side (C) using two 1½-inch nails. Nail through the Triangular Trim (D) into the Front (B).

7. Repeat steps 5 and 6 to attach the remaining Triangular Trim (D) to the opposite Side (C).

FINISHING

1. Fill any nail holes or imperfections in the wood with wood filler.

2. Thoroughly sand all parts of the table.

3. Stain or paint the finished table the color(s) of your choice. We chose a mauve paint for the top and triangular trims, and a pale green for the remaining portions of the table.

ATTACHING THE TABLE TO THE WALL

1. Cut one Support (E) from 1×2 pine, measuring 30 inches (or substitute any other material that is approximately the same length).

2. Attach the Support (E) to the wall ¾ inch lower than you want the table height to be, and centered horizontally where the table will hang. Given the length of the Support (E), you should be able to locate at least one stud. If your walls are plaster or concrete, you will need to use special screws for hanging.

3. It is helpful to have an assistant to mount the table. Position the table over the Support (E), making sure that it is in the correct horizontal position. Have your helper hold the table in place while you screw through the top of the table into the Support (E). Use three or four 1½-inch wood screws spaced evenly across the top. Countersink the screws.

4. Fill the screw holes with wood filler, and use matching paint or stain to cover the filled holes.

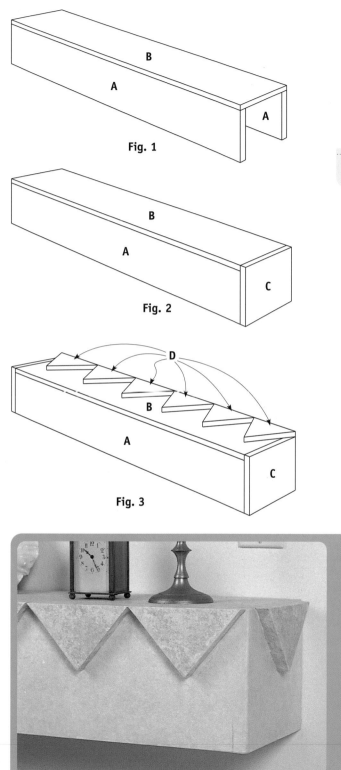

Fig. 1

Fig. 2

Fig. 3

Ottoman

You've long admired that high-priced ottoman/coffee table in the furniture store. Why not make your own? It's an easy project to construct, and you can pick and choose the fabric and paint colors to match your decor.

MATERIALS

28 linear feet of 2×4 pine

4-×8-foot sheet of ¾" plywood

15 linear feet of ¾"-wide beaded trim

1½ yards of 45" upholstery fabric

3½ yards of 1½" fringe (optional)

31" square of 2" thick foam

4 fabric-covered buttons (optional)

HARDWARE

8 corrugated metal fasteners

30 2½" wood screws

35 2" wood screws

60 wire brads

SPECIAL TOOLS & TECHNIQUES

Miter

Staple gun and staples

Bar clamps

CUTTING LIST

Code	Description	Qty.	Materials	Dimensions
A	Inner Frame	4	2×4 pine	29½" long
B	Inner Legs	4	2×4 pine	29½" long
C	Sides	4	¾" plywood	31"×16"
D	Trim	4	¾"-wide trim	cut to fit
E	Middle Frame	4	2×4 pine	31" long
F	Top	1	¾" plywood	31" square

CONSTRUCTING THE INNER FRAME

1. Cut four Inner Frames (A) from 2×4 pine, each measuring 29½ inches.

2. Miter the ends of each of the four Inner Frames (A) at opposing 45° angles.

3. Place the four Inner Frames (A) on a flat surface, mitered ends together, to form a 29½-inch square, as shown in figure 1. Hammer a corrugated metal fastener across each mitered joint to temporarily hold the frame together.

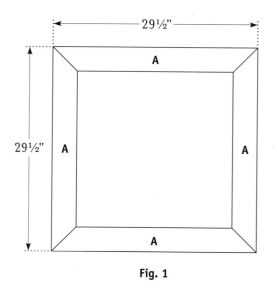

Fig. 1

4. Cut four Inner Legs (B) from 2×4 pine, each measuring 14½ inches.

5. Attach one Inner Leg (B) to the assembled frame, covering the outer edge of the mitered joint, as shown in figure 2. Make certain that the leg is exactly square to the inner frames. Screw through the Inner Frames (A) into the Inner Leg (B) using four 2½-inch screws on each joint. Don't be concerned if the structure is not very stable at this time—the stability will come when the sides are added.

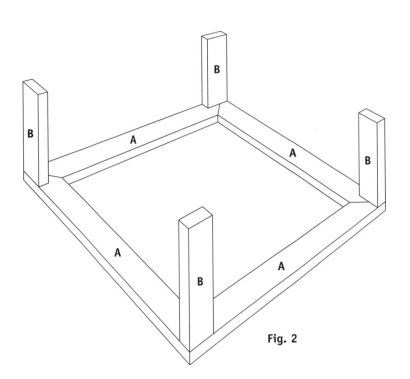

Fig. 2

ADDING THE SIDES

1. Cut four Sides (C) from ¾-inch plywood, each measuring 31×16 inches.

2. Bevel the 16-inch edges of each of the four Sides (C) at opposing 45° angles.

3. Lay one Side (C) with the bevels down. Referring to figure 3, mark a cutout on one 31-inch edge. Cut out along the marked lines.

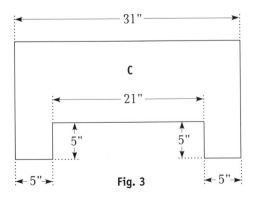

Fig. 3

4. Repeat step 3 to mark and cut out the same edge on each of the remaining three Sides (C).

5. Place the Inner Frame and Leg assembly (A and B) upside down on a level surface. Apply glue to the meeting edges, and fit the four Sides (C) (matching beveled edges and placing the cutout at the top) around the assembly, as shown in figure 4. Make certain that all of the mitered joints fit together perfectly along the entire length. Use bar clamps to hold the Sides (C) in place. Screw through the edges of the Sides (C) into the Inner Legs (B) and Inner Frame (A), using 2-inch screws spaced about 5 inches apart.

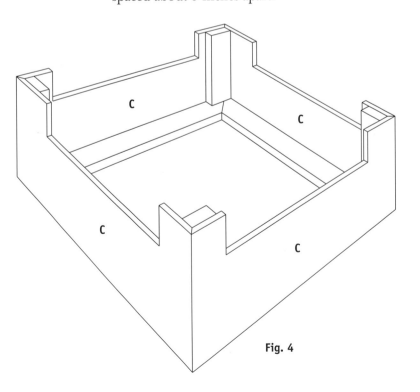

Fig. 4

ADDING THE TRIM

1. Miter lengths of ¾-inch beaded Trim (D) to fit around the lower cutout edges of the ottoman, as shown in figure 5. Notice that the Trim (D) is mitered across the width to fit around the cutout, and mitered on its edge to fit around the corners.

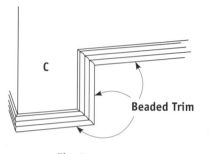

C

Beaded Trim

Fig. 5

2. Apply glue to the meeting surfaces, and attach the trim to the Sides (C) using small wire brads placed about every 3 inches.

CONSTRUCTING THE MIDDLE FRAME

1. Cut four Middle Frames (E) from 2×4 pine, each measuring 31 inches.

2. Miter each of the four Middle Frames (E) at opposing 45° angles.

3. Place the four Middle Frames (E) on a flat surface, mitered ends together, to form a 31-inch square, as for the Inner Frames (A) (see figure 1). Hammer a corrugated metal fastener across each mitered joint to temporarily hold the frame together.

4. Cut and piece together a strip of your chosen fabric 4 inches wide and 10½ feet long. This will be used to cover the outer edges of the Middle Frame (E).

5. Beginning at one corner, staple the fabric strip to the frame assembly so that 1 inch of fabric is on the top, and 3 inches overhangs the edges, as shown in figure 6. When you reach the end, fold the end of the strip under, and staple securely in place.

6. Turn the entire frame assembly over, pull the fabric around the outer edges, and staple the fabric to the opposite side of the frame.

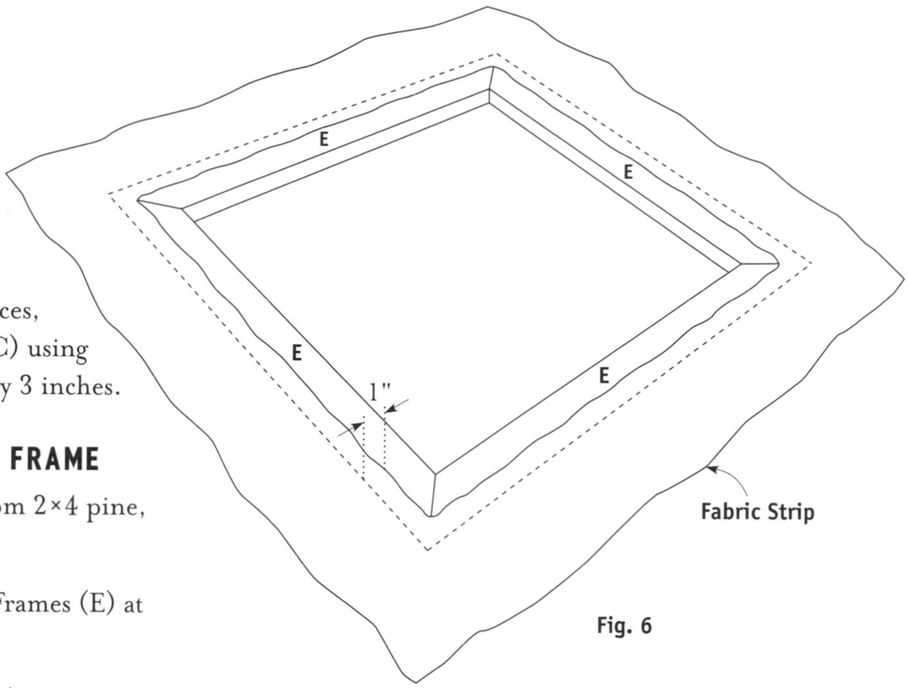

E

E

E

E

1"

Fabric Strip

Fig. 6

7. Add fringe at this point, if you wish. We stapled the fringe around the outer edges of the middle frame assembly.

MAKING THE TOP CUSHION

1. Cut a Top (F) from ¾-inch plywood, measuring 31 inches square.

2. Place a 31-inch square of 2-inch foam over the Top (F).

3. Cut a 38-inch square of your chosen fabric. Place the fabric, wrong side up, on a level surface.

4. Center the cushion and Top (F) upside down over the fabric square.

5. Pull the fabric tightly over the cushion and edge of the Top (F) and staple the fabric in place. Staple the center of each side first, then work out to each corner.

6. If you want to add buttons, follow the measurements given in figure 7 for positioning. Mark the button positions, and staple through the fabric and cushion on each of the marks. Then glue a button of your choice over each of the staples.

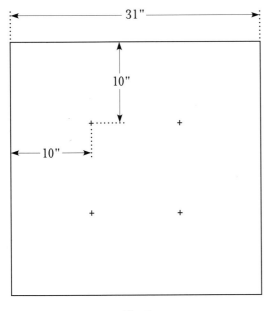

Fig. 7

FINISHING

1. Paint the frame assembly (sides and beaded trim) the color of your choice. We used a dark marbleizing kit (available at craft stores). Let the paint dry overnight.

2. Place the top cushion upside down and center the middle frame over it.

3. Screw through the middle frame into the Top (F) at all four corners and the center of each side, using 2-inch screws.

4. Center the painted frame assembly over the assembled top and middle frame. Screw through the Inner Frames (A) into the Middle Frames (E), using 2½-inch screws about every 8 inches.

Coatrack

Attach purchased gingerbread brackets to a premade porch post to create a decorative and functional coatrack for your hallway. The entire project can be completed in just one day!

MATERIALS

1 premade porch post, at least 6' long

3 linear feet of 1×3 pine

4 linear feet of 1×4 pine

4 gingerbread brackets, each measuring
6¼"× 8½" on the straight sides

1 fence post finial

HARDWARE

30 1½" (4d) finish nails

15 1¼" (3d) finish nails

4 metal coat hooks

CUTTING LIST

Code	Description	Qty.	Materials	Dimensions
A	Post	1	porch post	at least 6' long
B	Trim	4	1×3 pine	6½" long
C	Long Base	1	1×4 pine	24" long
D	Short Base	2	1×4 pine	10¼" long

CONSTRUCTING THE COATRACK

1. Cut the Post (A) to the length you desire—we
cut ours to 65 inches. First cut the top of the
post so the upper square with flat sides will measure 5 inches. Then cut the other end of the
post to the desired length.

2. Fill any cracks or imperfections with wood
filler, and thoroughly sand the entire post.

3. Cut four Trims (B) from 1×3 pine, each measuring 6½ inches.

4. Center one Trim (B) on one flat side of the
Post (A), flush with the bottom of the Post (A),
as shown in figure 1. Apply glue to the meeting
surfaces, and nail through the Trim (B) into the
Post (A) using three 1½-inch nails.

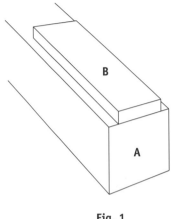

Fig. 1

5. Center one 6¼-inch side of a gingerbread
bracket over the Trim (B), flush with the bottom of the Trim (B), as shown in figure 2.
Apply glue to the meeting surfaces, and nail
through the bracket into the Trim (B) using
four 1½-inch nails.

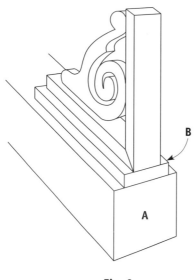

Fig. 2

6. Repeat steps 4 and 5 three times to attach the remaining Trims (B) and gingerbread brackets to the Post (A).

7. Cut one Long Base (C) from 1×4 pine, measuring 24 inches long.

8. Place the Post (A) on a flat surface, so that the Trims (B) overhang the work surface. Center the Long Base (C) over opposing 8½-inch sides of the gingerbread brackets, as shown in figure 3. Apply glue to the meeting surfaces, and nail through the Long Base (C) into the gingerbread brackets and the Post (A). Use four 1¼-inch nails on each joint.

9. Cut two Short Bases (D) from 1×4 pine, each measuring 10¼ inches long.

10. Center one Short Base (D) over one of the gingerbread brackets, perpendicular to the Long Base, as shown in figure 3. Apply glue to the meeting surfaces, and nail through the Short Base (D) into the brackets using four 1¼-inch nails.

11. Repeat step 10 to attach the remaining Short Base (D) over the remaining gingerbread brackets.

FINISHING

1. Mark the center top of the Post (A) and screw in a fence post finial.

2. Fill all remaining nail holes, cracks, and crevices with wood filler.

3. Sand all parts of the coatrack that remain unsanded.

4. Stain or paint your coatrack the color of your choice. We painted the coatrack white, and then decorated the individual parts with different designs using a paint pen.

5. Install four coat hooks—one on each flat side of the top of the coatrack.

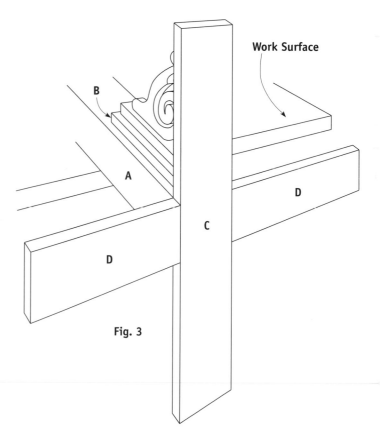

Fig. 3

Shell Mirror

Are you trying to decide what to do with all those shells you collected on vacation? Take them out of the box in your closet and create a unique hall mirror. It is sure to brighten up a neglected spot in your hall—and to be a constant reminder of your fun on the beach.

MATERIALS

4-×4-foot sheet of ¾" plywood

5 linear feet of 1×8 pine

8 linear feet of 1×4 pine

5 linear feet of 1×2 pine

Mirror, approximately 24½"×34" *

Construction glue

HARDWARE

8 corrugated metal fasteners

40 1¼" wood screws

Picture hanging wire kit*

Picture hangers

SPECIAL TOOLS & TECHNIQUES

Bar or pipe clamps

CUTTING LIST

Code	Description	Qty.	Materials	Dimensions
A	Top	1	¾" plywood	10¾"×36"
B	Bottom	1	¾" plywood	6½"×36"
C	Sides	2	1×8 pine	30" long
D	Side Frame	2	1×4 pine	38" long
E	Top/Bottom Frame	2	1×2 pine	25½" long

*Note on Materials: We suggest that you purchase a mirror after you have assembled the mirror frame. That way, you can be certain that all of your measurements are correct, and that the mirror will fit the frame you have built. When specifying the size of the mirror, we suggest that you carefully measure the inner frames, and order a mirror at least ¼ inch smaller in each dimension than your opening.

When purchasing the picture hanging wire kit, buy one that will support your finished mirror. With the shells attached, ours was very heavy, and we used two 50-pound hangers, and wire that would support the same weight.

TRANSFERRING THE PATTERNS

1. Enlarge the pattern for the Top (A) (shown in figure 1) to full size on butcher paper or paper bags, and cut the pattern out carefully.

2. Tape the enlarged paper pattern to ¾-inch plywood, and trace around the pattern with a pencil.

3. Remove the paper pattern, and cut out the Top (A).

4. Repeat steps 1 through 3 to enlarge the pattern for the Bottom (B), transfer the pattern to ¾-inch plywood, and cut out the Bottom (B). See figure 1.

CONSTRUCTING THE MIRROR FRAME

1. Cut two Sides (C) from 1×8 plywood, each measuring 30 inches.

2. Position the two Sides (C) on their wide surfaces, parallel to each other and approximately 18 inches apart.

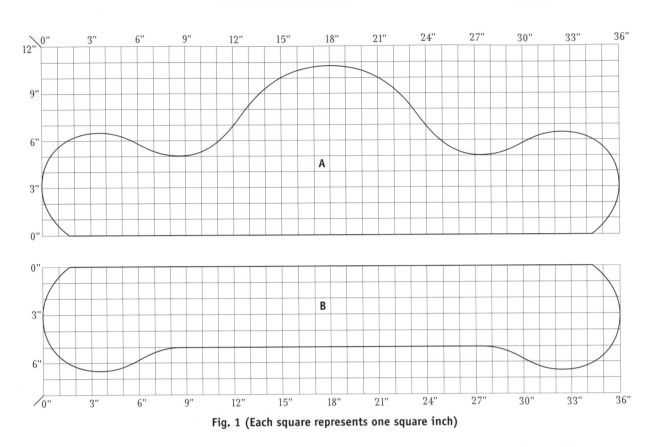

Fig. 1 (Each square represents one square inch)

3. Position the Top (A) at the ends of the two Sides (C), as shown in figure 2.

4. Place the Bottom (B) at the opposite ends of the two Sides (C), as shown in figure 2.

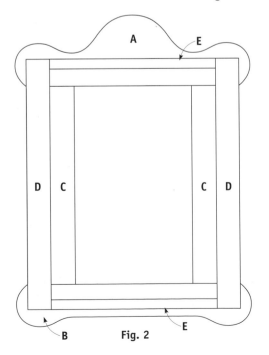

Fig. 2

5. Measure the center opening (where the mirror will fit) in several places, to make absolutely certain that both the distance from Top (A) to Bottom (B) and the distance from Side (C) to Side (C) are equal at all points. Apply glue to the meeting surfaces, and clamp the Top (A), Bottom (B), and two Sides (C) together.

6. Use two corrugated metal fasteners across each of the joints to hold the pieces together temporarily.

ADDING THE INNER FRAMES

1. Cut two Side Frames (D) from 1×4 pine, each measuring 38 inches.

2. With the assembly (Top [A], Bottom [B], and Sides [C]) on the working surface and the corrugated fasteners visible, place one Side Frame (D) over one Side (C), flush with the outer edges, as shown in figure 2. The ends of the Side Frame (D) should extend over the Top (A) and Bottom (B) by approximately 4 inches.

3. Apply glue to the meeting surfaces, and screw through the Side Frame (D) into the Side (C), using 1¼-inch screws spaced about every 5 inches. Use two screws through the ends of the Side Frame (D) into both the Top (A) and Bottom (B).

4. Repeat steps 2 and 3 to attach the remaining Side Frame (D) to the opposite side of the mirror, again screwing through the Side Frame (D) into the Top (A), Bottom (B), and Side (C).

5. Cut two Top/Bottom Frames (E) from 1×2 pine, each measuring 25½ inches.

6. With the front assembly (Top [A], Bottom [B], and Sides [C]) still on the working surface, place one Top/Bottom Frame (E) over the Top (A) between the two Side Frames (D), flush with the ends of the side frames (D), as shown in figure 2. Trim the Top/Bottom Frame (E) to fit, if necessary.

7. Apply glue to the meeting surfaces, and screw through the Top/Bottom Frame (E) into the Top (A), using 1¼-inch screws spaced about every 5 inches.

8. Repeat steps 6 and 7 to attach the remaining Top/Bottom Frame (E) to the Bottom (B), between the opposite ends of the Side Frames (D).

FINISHING

1. Fill any cracks or crevices with wood filler, and sand all parts of the completed mirror.

2. Paint or stain the mirror the color of your choice. We whitewashed our mirror with a thin coat of white paint, then used construction glue to attach shells over the entire surface of the mirror. If you plan to glue items to the front,

install the mirror and attach the hanging wire (steps 3 and 4 below) before you glue.

3. With the mirror assembly face down, apply construction glue to the inside opening between the mirror and frame pieces. Set the mirror (mirror side down) over the glue, and place books or any other weights evenly over the back of the mirror. Let the construction glue set up overnight.

4. Attach the hanging wire following the manufacturer's instructions.

Grandmother Clock

This colorful clock is a whimsical addition to almost any room in the house. We placed it in a hallway, but it would be a cheerful accessory in a kitchen, bedroom, or even a large bath. The clock mechanism is battery-operated and costs less than ten dollars.

MATERIALS

4-×8-foot sheet of ¾" plywood

2 linear feet of 1×8 pine

7 linear feet of 1½"-diameter fluted wooden curtain rod

2 linear feet of 1×2 pine

2 linear feet of 1×1 pine

5" diameter circle of ¼" plywood

8 wooden curtain rod finials

1 8"-diameter battery-operated clock with bezel

HARDWARE

120 1½" (4d) finish nails

5 1¼" (3d) finish nails

15 1½" wood screws

1 1" (2d) finish nail

1 antique doorknob (or any drawer pull of your choice)

2 brass cup hooks

SPECIAL TOOLS & TECHNIQUES

Miter

CUTTING LIST

Code	Description	Qty.	Materials	Dimensions
A	Base Front/Back	2	¾" plywood	16¼"×9½"
B	Base Sides	2	¾" plywood	10"×9½"
C	Drawer Front	1	1×8 pine	12" long
D	Base Top/Bottom	2	¾" plywood	11½"×16¼"
E	Middle Front	1	¾" plywood	33½"×16¼"
F	Middle Sides	2	¾" plywood	33½"×2"
G	Middle Top/Bottom	2	¾" plywood	16¼"×2¾"
H	Case Front/Back	2	¾" plywood	14¾"×16¼"
I	Case Sides	2	¾" plywood	10¼"×10"
J	Case Top	1	¾" plywood	10"×16¼"
K	Column	2	curtain rod	37" long
L	Column Support	2	1×2 pine	6¼" long
M	Pendulum Support	1	1×2 pine	10" long
N	Pendulum Rod	1	1×1 pine	22½" long
O	Pendulum Circle	1	¼" plywood	5" dia. circle

BUILDING THE CLOCK BASE

1. The clock consists of three sections that are built separately and then joined together: the top clock case, the middle section, and the base. Cut two Base Front/Backs (A) from ¾-inch plywood, each measuring 16¼×9½ inches.

2. Cut two Base Sides (B) from ¾-inch plywood, each measuring 10×9½ inches.

3. Place the two Base Sides (B) on a level surface, parallel to each other and 14¾ inches apart. Apply glue to the meeting surfaces, and place one Base Front/Back (A) over the edges of the two Base Sides (B), as shown in figure 1. Nail

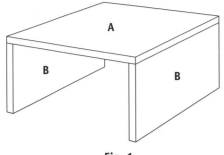

Fig. 1

through the Base Front/Back (A) into the edges of the Base Sides (B) using four 1½-inch nails evenly spaced along each joint.

4. Cut one mock Drawer Front (C) from 1×8 pine, measuring 12 inches.

5. Apply glue to the meeting surfaces, and center the Drawer Front (C) over the remaining Base Front/Back (A), as shown in figure 2. Nail through the Drawer Front (C) into the Base Front/Back (A) using three 1½-inch nails on each 12-inch side.

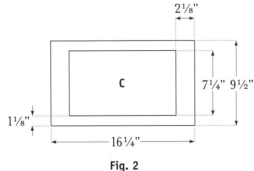

Fig. 2

6. Turn the assembly upside down, and repeat step 3 to attach the remaining Base Front/Back (A) (with attached Drawer Front [C]) to the assembly.

7. Cut two Base Top/Bottoms (D) from ¾-inch plywood, each measuring 11½×16¼ inches.

8. Place the assembly on a level surface with the

Drawer Front (C) facing you. Apply glue to the meeting surfaces, and nail one Base Top/ Bottom (D) over the edges of the Base Sides (B) and Base Front/Back (A), as shown in figure 3. Nail through the Base Top/Bottom (D) into the Base Sides and Front/Back (A and B) using four 1½-inch nails on each side.

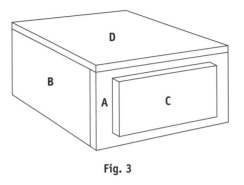

Fig. 3

9. Set the remaining Base Top/Bottom (D) aside. It will be added during the final assembly.

BUILDING THE MIDDLE SECTION

1. Cut one Middle Front (E) from ¾-inch plywood, measuring 33½×16¼ inches.

2. Cut two Middle Sides (F) from ¾-inch plywood, measuring 33½×2 inches.

3. Place the two Middle Sides (F) on edge on a level surface, parallel to each other and 14¾ inches apart. Apply glue to the meeting surfaces, and place the Middle Front (E) over the edges of the Middle Sides (F), as shown in figure 4. Nail through the Middle Front (E) into the edges of the Middle Sides (F), using 1½-inch nails spaced about every 5 inches.

4. Cut two Middle Top/Bottoms (G) from ¾-inch plywood, each measuring 16¼×2¾ inches.

5. Apply glue to the meeting surfaces, and attach

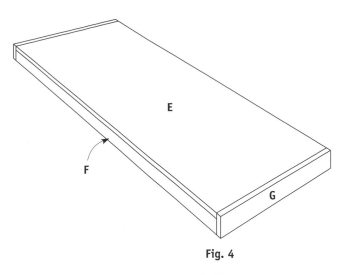

Fig. 4

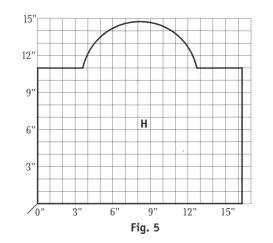

Fig. 5

one Middle Top/Bottom (G) over the edges of the two Middle Sides (F) and Middle Front (E), as shown in figure 4. Nail through the Middle Top/Bottom (G) into the edges of the two Middle Front and Sides (E and F) using two 1½-inch nails on the Middle Sides (F) and three nails on the Middle Front (E).

6. Turn the assembly around, and repeat step 5 to attach the remaining Middle Top/Bottom (G).

BUILDING THE CLOCK CASE

1. The last section is the clock case, which will house the battery-operated clock. Cut two Case Front/Backs (H) from ¾-inch plywood, each measuring 14¾ × 16¼ inches.

2. Enlarge the pattern shown in figure 5 and transfer it to the two Case Front/Backs (H). Designate one as the Case Front (H) and one as the Case Back (H). The clock opening should be transferred to only the Case Front (H), to accommodate the battery-operated clock. Check to make certain that the clockwork portion of the clock you purchased will fit snugly into the opening; alter the size of the opening if necessary.

3. Cut two Case Sides (I) from ¾-inch plywood, each measuring 10¼ × 10 inches.

4. Cut one Case Top (J) from ¾-inch plywood, measuring 10 × 16¼ inches.

5. Place the two Case Sides (I) on a level surface, parallel to each other and 14¾ inches apart. Apply glue to the meeting surfaces, and place the Case Top (J) over the edges of the two Case Sides (I) as you did in figure 1. Nail through the Case Top (J) into the edges of the Case Sides (I). Use four 1½-inch nails evenly spaced along each joint.

6. Apply glue to the meeting surfaces and center the Case Front/Back (H) over the Case Sides and Top (I and J), as shown in figure 6. Nail through the Case Front (H) into the Case Sides and Top (I and J) using 1½-inch nails spaced every 5 inches.

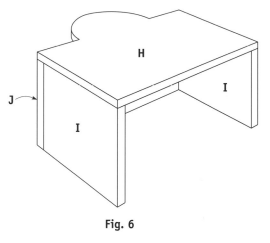

Fig. 6

7. Turn the assembly upside down, and repeat step 6 to attach the remaining Case Back (H) to the assembly.

CONNECTING THE THREE SECTIONS

1. Place the clock base, middle, and case on their sides, with the fronts facing away from you and the backs flush with each other, as shown in figure 7. Make certain that each of the pieces is perfectly aligned with the adjoining one. Apply glue to the meeting surfaces, and screw through the Middle Top (G) into the edge of the Case Back (H), using four or five 1½-inch screws. Apply glue to the meeting surfaces and screw through the opposite Middle Top (G) into the Base Top (D), using four or five 1½-inch screws.

2. Cut two Columns (K) from 1½-inch-diameter fluted wooden curtain rods, each measuring 37 inches.

3. Cut two Column Supports (L) from 1×2 pine, each measuring 6¼ inches.

4. Miter each of the Column Supports (L) at opposing 45° angles, as shown in Figure 8.

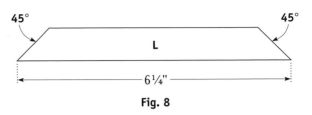

Fig. 8

5. Turn the clock assembly around so the front is facing you. Insert one Column (K) inside the front bottom corner of the clock case, and adjust it so that the opposite end of the Column (K) is tight against the Base Top (D).

6. Place one Column Support (L) inside the clock case across the Column (K). If necessary, trim the Column Support (L) so that it fits snugly against the Case Front (H), the Column (K), and the Case Side (I). To hold the Column (K) tightly in place, apply glue to the meeting surfaces, and nail through the Case

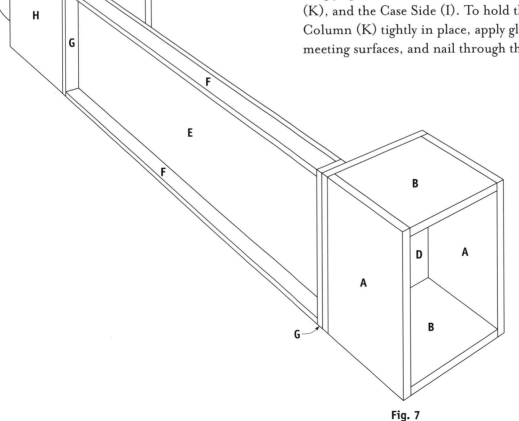

Fig. 7

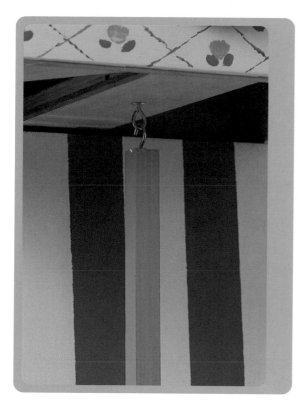

Front and Side (H and I) into the Column Support (L), using two 1¼-inch nails.

7. Make sure that the opposite end of the Column (K) is exactly square against the Base Top (D), and screw through the Base Top (D) into the center bottom of the Column (K) using a 1½-inch screw.

8. Turn the assembly to its other side, and repeat steps 5 through 7 to attach the remaining Column (K) and Column Support (L) to the opposite side of the clock.

9. Cut one Pendulum Support (M) from 1×2 pine, measuring 10 inches.

10. Apply glue to the meeting surfaces and fit the Pendulum Support (M) between the two Case Front/Backs (H) at the center bottom of the clock case. Nail through both Case

Front/Backs (H) into the Pendulum Support (M) using two 1½-inch nails on each joint.

11. Drill a hole through the center of the Drawer Front (C) and Base Front (A), just large enough to accommodate the doorknob or drawer pull that you have selected. Install it on the Drawer Front (C).

12. Locate the remaining Base Top/Bottom (D) that was set aside. Apply glue to the meeting surfaces, and attach the Base Bottom (D) over the bottom of the assembly. Nail through the Base Bottom (D) into the Base Sides and Front/Back (A and B) using four 1½-inch nails on each joint.

MAKING THE PENDULUM

1. Cut one Pendulum Rod (N) from 1×1 pine, measuring 22½ inches.

2. Cut one Pendulum Circle (O) from ¼-inch plywood, measuring 5 inches in diameter.

3. Place the center of the Pendulum Circle (O) on top of the Pendulum Rod (N), and 1 inch

5. Paint or stain the clock and pendulum the color of your choice. We painted our clock with a different pattern on each of the individual surfaces. Refer to the photograph or choose your own patterns and colors. See page 24 for more information on decorative painting.

6. Install the battery-operated clock in the opening of the clock case. This clock is one that is simply hung on the wall, and only required inserting the clock into the hole.

7. Screw one brass cup hook into the end of the pendulum, and another into the center of the Pendulum Support (M). Hang the pendulum on the cup hook.

from the end of the Pendulum Rod (N). Apply glue to the meeting surfaces, and nail through the center of the Pendulum Circle (O) into the Pendulum Rod (N) using a 1-inch finish nail.

FINISHING THE CLOCK

1. Fill any holes, cracks, or crevices with wood filler.

2. Thoroughly sand all areas of the completed clock.

3. Attach a curtain rod finial in each of the four corners of the Base Bottom (D).

4. Attach a curtain rod finial in each of the four corners of the Case Top (J).

Coffee Table

This simple-to-make coffee table is guaranteed to perk up the living room, and can be coordinated to any color scheme. The decorative trim pieces are painted wooden drawer pulls.

MATERIALS

35 linear feet of 1×4 pine

2 linear feet of 1×6 pine

3 linear feet of 1×8 pine

Premade pine laminate, 21½"×45½", approx. ¾" thick

28 square wooden drawer pulls

HARDWARE

85 1½" (4d) finish nails

15 2" (6d) finish nails

30 1⅝" wood screws

SPECIAL TOOLS & TECHNIQUES

Bar clamps

Miter

CUTTING LIST

Code	Description	Qty.	Materials	Dimensions
A	Leg Side	4	1×4 pine	17" long
B	Small Base	4	1×6 pine	5½" long
C	Large Base	4	1×8 pine	7¼" long
D	Short Base Side	2	1×4 pine	21½" long
E	Long Base Side	2	1×4 pine	47" long
F	Center Top	1	laminate	21½" × 45½"
G	Long Top Side	2	1×4 pine	52½" long
H	Short Top Side	2	1×4 pine	28½" long

CONSTRUCTING THE LEGS

1. Cut four Leg Sides (A) from 1×4 pine, each measuring 17 inches.

2. Assemble the four Leg Sides (A), overlapping each piece in rotation, as shown in figure 1. With the four sides (A) in position, the leg should measure 4¼ inches wide on all sides. Apply glue to the meeting surfaces, and nail all four sides (A) along their entire length. Use 1½-inch nails, spacing nails about 6 inches apart.

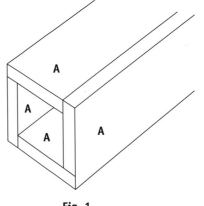

Fig. 1

3. Cut four Small Bases (B) from 1×6 pine, each measuring 5½ inches.

4. Cut four Large Bases (C) from 1×8 pine, each measuring 7¼ inches.

5. Center one Small Base (B) over one Large Base (C), as shown in figure 2. Apply glue to the meeting surfaces, and nail the two pieces together using four 1½-inch nails.

6. Repeat step 5 three times, using the remaining Small Bases (B) and Large Bases (C).

7. Center one base assembly (B and C) on top of one leg assembly, as shown in figure 3. The Large Base (C) should be facing up with the small base (B) below it. Wipe glue on the meet-

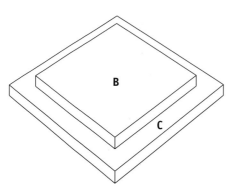

Fig. 2

Fig. 3

ing surfaces, and attach the base assembly to the leg using four 2-inch nails.

8. Repeat step 7 three times to attach the remaining base assemblies to the remaining three legs.

CONSTRUCTING THE BASE FRAME

1. Cut two Short Base Sides (D) from 1×4 pine, each measuring 21½ inches.

2. Cut two Long Base Sides (E) from 1×4 pine, each measuring 47 inches.

3. Place the two Short Base Sides (D) on edge, parallel to each other and 45½ inches apart. Place the two Long Base Sides (E) over the ends of the two Short Base Sides (D) to form a rectangle, as shown in figure 4.

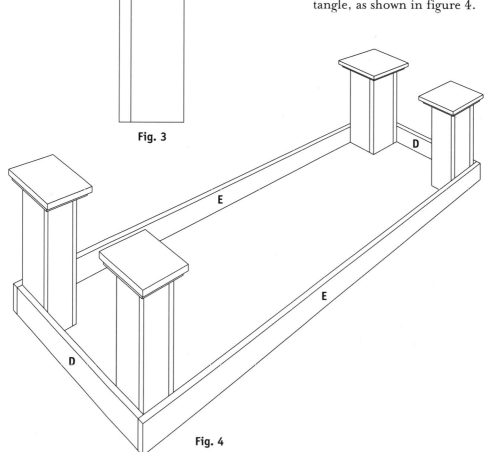

Fig. 4

G

H

F

G

H

52½"

28½"

Fig. 5

the Center Top (F), as shown in figure 5. Place the two Short Top Sides (H) on the short sides of the laminate Center Top (F). Apply glue to the meeting surfaces. Hold the assembled top in place using bar clamps, and set aside to dry for 24 hours.

5. Center the tabletop over the base. Apply glue to the meeting surfaces, and nail through the Sides (G and H) into the Base Sides (D and E) using 1½-inch nails spaced every 5 inches.

4. Place the legs upside down inside each corner of the assembled base frame, as shown in figure 4. Apply glue to the meeting surfaces, and attach the legs to the base frame using two 1⅝-inch screws on each side of each leg. Screw through the base frame into the legs.

CONSTRUCTING THE TABLETOP

1. Trim the laminated Center Top (F) to 21½ × 45½ inches.

2. Cut two Long Top Sides (G) from 1×4 pine, each measuring 52½ inches.

3. Cut two Short Top Sides (H) from 1×4 pine, each measuring 28½ inches.

4. Place the Center Top (F) on a level surface. Place the two Long Top Sides (G) on the long sides of

FINISHING

1. Fill any holes, cracks, or crevices with wood filler.

2. Thoroughly sand all areas of the completed coffee table.

3. Paint or stain the coffee table with the color of your choice. We chose a clear stain and sealer.

4. Paint 28 drawer pulls the color of your choice. Here, we've used a salmon color.

5. Referring to figure 6, drill 10 holes on each of the Long Base Sides (E) and four holes on each of the Short Base Sides (D). Insert the drawer pull screws through the holes and attach the drawer pulls.

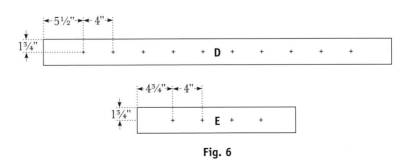

5½" 4"

1¾"

D

4¾" 4"

1¾"

E

Fig. 6

Wall Ledge

This simple ledge is one of our favorite projects, and can be constructed in only a few hours. Top it with anything that needs a home—from a row of picture frames to your collection of candlesticks—and your friends will think you hired a master decorator!

MATERIALS

4 linear feet of 1×6 pine

4 linear feet of 2×4 pine

4 linear feet of ¾"-wide cove molding

3 linear feet of 1×2 pine

HARDWARE

10 2" wood screws

20 1⅝" wood screws

15 1" (2d) finish nails

SPECIAL TOOLS & TECHNIQUES

Miter

CUTTING LIST

Code	Description	Qty.	Materials	Dimensions
A	Top Ledge	1	1×6 pine	36" long
B	Front Support	1	2×4 pine	34" long
C	Side Support	2	2×4 pine	4½" long
D	Long Trim	1	¾"-wide cove molding	35½" long
E	Short Trim	2	¾"-wide cove molding	5¼" long
F	Ledge Mount	1	1×2 pine	25" long

MAKING THE LEDGE

1. Cut one Top Ledge (A) from 1×6 pine, measuring 36 inches.

2. Cut one Front Support (B) from 2×4 pine, measuring 34 inches.

3. Miter both ends of the Front Support (B) at opposing 45° angles, as shown in figure 1.

4. Cut two Side Supports (C) from 2×4 pine, each measuring 4½ inches. Miter one end of both Side Supports (C) at a 45° angle, as shown in figure 2.

5. Using figure 3 as a guide, place the Front Support (B) face down on a level surface. Place a Side Support (C) at both ends of the Front Support (B), so that the miters of the Front Support (B) meet the Side Support (C) miters. Apply glue to the meeting surfaces. Connect the Side Supports (C) to the ends of the Front Support (B), using two 2-inch screws.

6. Place the Top Ledge (A) over the assembled Front and Side Supports (B and C), as shown in figure 4. The edge of the Top Ledge (A) should overhang the ends and front sides of the Side Supports (C). Apply glue to the meeting surfaces, and screw through the face of the Top Ledge (A) into the Front and Side Supports (B and C), using 1⅝-inch screws.

7. Cut one Ledge Mount (F) from 1×2 pine, measuring 25 inches. This board will be

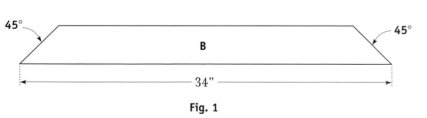

Fig. 1

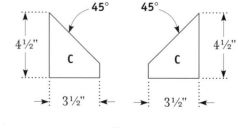

Fig. 2

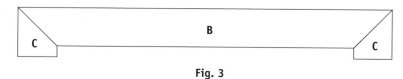

Fig. 3

mounted to the wall with screws, and the ledge will be attached to it.

ADDING THE TRIM

1. Cut one Long Trim (D) from ¾-inch-wide cove molding, measuring 35½ inches.

2. Miter both ends of the Long Trim (D) at opposing 45° angles.

3. Apply glue to the meeting surfaces, and nail the Long Trim (D) to the front of the assembly, just below the Top Ledge (A), using 1-inch nails spaced about every 4 inches.

4. Cut two Short Trims (E) from ¾-inch-wide cove molding, each measuring 5¼ inches long.

5. Miter one end of each of the two Short Trims (E) at a 45° angle.

6. Apply glue to the meeting surfaces, and nail one Short Trim (E) to the side of the assembly, just below the end of the Top Ledge (A). Nail through the Short Trim (E) into the Side Supports (C) using three 1-inch nails.

7. Repeat step 6 to attach the remaining Short Trim (E) to the other side of the assembly.

FINISHING

1. Fill any cracks, crevices, or screw holes with wood filler.

2. Thoroughly sand all surfaces of the completed ledge.

3. Seal and paint or stain your completed ledge the color of your choice.

4. Locate wall studs and attach the Ledge Mount (F) to the wall using 1⅝-inch screws. Make certain that the Ledge Mount (F) is perfectly level, then set the assembled ledge on top of the Ledge Mount (F), flush against the wall. Secure the ledge to the Ledge Mount (F) by screwing through the ledge into the Ledge Mount (F) using 1⅝-inch screws about every 10 inches.

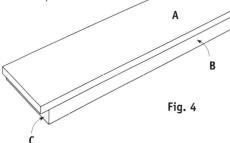

Fig. 4

Cedar Keepsake Box

Who can't use this pretty box around the house? It's the ideal container for treasured family heirlooms—tiny baby shoes, cherished letters, and old photographs—and is the perfect size for storing cigars. The addition of a tray makes it an ideal jewelry box.

MATERIALS

4 linear feet of 1×6 cedar

2 linear feet of 1×10 cedar

3 linear feet of 1×3 cedar

1 linear feet of 1×8 cedar

Note: Pine may be substituted for cedar

HARDWARE

Approximately 40 1½" (4d) finish nails

2 2" hinges

CUTTING LIST

Code	Description	Qty.	Materials	Dimensions
A	Box Side	2	1×6 cedar	7¾" long
B	Box Front/Back	2	1×6 cedar	10" long
C	Box Top/Bottom	2	1×10 cedar	10" long
D	Tray Side	2	1×3 cedar	6" long
E	Tray Front/Back	2	1×3 cedar	7¾" long
F	Tray Bottom	1	1×8 cedar	6"×6¼"

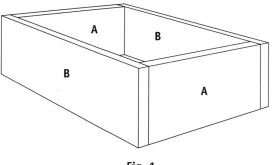

Fig. 1

MAKING THE BOX

1. Cut two Box Sides (A) from 1×6 cedar, each measuring 7¾ inches.

2. Cut two Box Front/Backs (B) from 1×6 cedar, each measuring 10 inches.

3. Place two Box Front/Backs (B) on edge parallel to each other and 7 inches apart. Place the ends of the two Box Sides (A) between the Box Front/Backs (B), as shown in figure 1. Apply glue to the meeting surfaces. Nail through the Box Front/Backs (B) into the ends of the Box Sides (A), using three 1½-inch nails on each joint.

4. Cut two Box Top/Bottoms (C) from 1×10 cedar, each measuring 10 inches.

5. Place one Top/Bottom (C) over the edges of the Box Sides (A) and Box Front/Backs (B), as shown in figure 2. Apply glue to the meeting surfaces. Nail through the Top/Bottom (C) into the edges of the Box Sides (A) and Box Front/Backs (B), using 1½-inch nails.

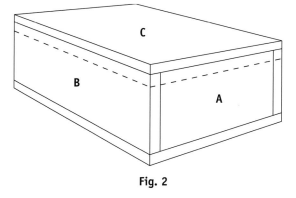

Fig. 2

6. Turn the Box assembly upside down, and repeat step 5 to attach the remaining Box Top/Bottom (C).

7. Carefully mark around the perimeter of the box, 1½ inches from one Box Top/Bottom (C), as shown in figure 2. Cut carefully along the marked lines through the box to create two pieces.

MAKING THE TRAY

1. Cut two Tray Sides (D) from 1×3 cedar, each measuring 6 inches.

2. Cut two Tray Front/Backs (E) from 1×3 cedar, each measuring 7 ¾ inches.

3. Place two Tray Front/Backs (E) on edge parallel to each other and 7 inches apart. Place the ends of the two Tray Sides (D) between the Tray Front Backs (E), as shown in figure 3. Apply glue to the meeting surfaces, and nail through the Tray Front/Backs (E) into the ends of the Tray Sides (D), using two 1½-inch nails on each joint.

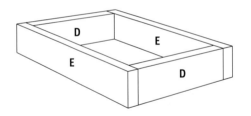

Fig. 3

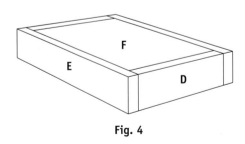

Fig. 4

4. Cut one Tray Bottom (F) from 1×8 cedar, measuring 6×6¼ inches. This piece will fit inside the Tray Sides and Front/Backs (D and E), as shown in figure 4. Apply glue to the

meeting surfaces, and nail through the Tray Sides (D) and Tray Front/Backs (E) into the ends and edges of the Tray Bottom (F), using 1½-inch nails spaced 2 inches apart.

FINISHING

1. Fill any cracks, crevices, or screw holes with wood filler.

2. Thoroughly sand all surfaces of the completed cedar box.

3. Seal and paint or stain your completed cedar box the color of your choice.

4. Attach 2-inch hinges to the lid and box.

Footstool

Who says a footstool has to be boring? This perky upholstered stool can hold its own anywhere in your home. Placed in front of a favorite easy chair, it's a great place to prop your feet—with enough room left over to hold a cup of tea. It also works well tucked underneath our Wall Table (see page 29).

MATERIALS

5 linear feet of 2×4 pine

3 linear feet of 1×12 pine

11"×17" piece of 4" thick foam padding

4 fence post finials, approx. 7¾" long and 5" in diameter, with screws in ends

1½" yards of 45" upholstery fabric

37"×30" piece of quilt batting

HARDWARE

4 corrugated metal fasteners

50 1½" finish nails

SPECIAL TOOLS & TECHNIQUES

Miter

Staple gun

CUTTING LIST

Code	Description	Qty.	Materials	Dimensions
A	Long Inner Sides	2	2×4 pine	17" long
B	Short Inner Sides	2	2×4 pine	11¼" long
C	Top/Bottom	2	1×12 pine	17" long
D	Legs	4	fence post finials	7¾" long and 5" dia. at top

BUILDING THE FOOTSTOOL

1. Cut two Long Inner Sides (A) from 2×4 pine, each measuring 17 inches.

2. Miter each end of both Long Inner Sides (A) at opposing 45° angles.

3. Cut two Short Inner Sides (B) from 2×4 pine, each measuring 11¼ inches.

4. Miter each end of both Short Inner Sides (B) at opposing 45° angles.

5. Place the two Long Inner Sides (A) on a level surface, parallel to each other and 4 inches apart. The 10-inch edges should be facing each other, as shown in figure 1. Place the two Short Inner Sides (B) between the ends of the Long Inner Sides (A), matching miters. Secure the joints temporarily with a corrugated metal fastener across each joint.

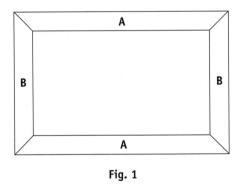

Fig. 1

6. Cut two Top/Bottoms (C) from 1×12 pine, each measuring 17 inches. Designate one piece as Top (C) and one as Bottom (C).

7. Place the Top (C) over the Long and Short Inner Sides (A and B), as shown in figure 2. Nail through the Top (C) into the Long and Short Inner Sides (A and B), using 1½-inch nails spaced every 4 inches.

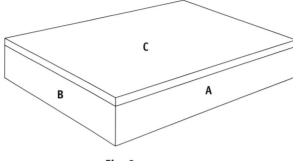

Fig. 2

UPHOLSTERING THE FOOTSTOOL

1. Apply glue on the Top (C), and place the 11×17-inch piece of 4-inch-thick foam on the Top (C).

2. Wrap the top and sides of the entire assembly with a thin layer of quilt batting. Staple it in place through the batting into the Long and Short Inner Sides (A and B).

3. Cut a rectangle from upholstery fabric measuring 37×30 inches.

4. Center the upholstery fabric over the batting, wrap the fabric over the edge of the footstool bottom, and staple it to the underside. You can minimize the number of wrinkles if you first staple the center of one side, then the center of the opposite side, then work your way out to the corners. Smooth the fabric as you go. Staple the centers of the remaining sides, and again work your way to the corners. Be generous with the staples; use enough to keep the fabric from puckering along the sides. Finish the corners as you would the sheets on a hospital bed, then staple the fabric in place.

5. Wrap the top and sides of the Bottom (C) with a thin layer of quilt batting. Staple the batting in place through the batting into the underside of the Bottom (C).

6. Cut a rectangle from upholstery fabric measuring 21×17 inches.

7. Center the upholstery fabric over the batting, wrap the fabric over the edge of the footstool bottom, and staple it to the underside.

FINISHING

1. The fence post finials will be used as legs for the footstool. Fill any cracks or crevices in the finials with wood filler, then sand them smooth.

2. Paint or stain the finials with the color of your choice. We chose a bright white paint.

3. Place the top assembly (with foam and upholstery) upside down on a flat surface. Place the upholstered Bottom (C) on top of it, matching sides. Nail through the fabric-covered Bottom (C) into the Long and Short Sides (A and B), using 1½-inch nails every 4 inches around the edges.

4. Measure 2¾ inches in both directions from each corner, as shown in figure 3. Mark the measurement, and screw in the four finial legs at the marked points.

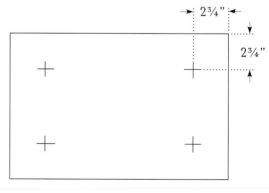

Fig. 3

Wastebasket

Here's an easy (and handsome) alternative to those unattractive plastic wastebaskets. It can be built from just a few feet of pine, rope molding, and some drawer pulls. Paint and a little imagination will transform the wastebasket into a one-of-kind decorative accent.

MATERIALS

6 linear feet of 1×12 pine

5 linear feet of ¾"-wide rope molding

4 1½"-diameter round drawer pulls

HARDWARE

30 1½" (4d) finish nails

20 1" (2d) finish nails

SPECIAL TOOLS & TECHNIQUES

Miter

CUTTING LIST

Code	Description	Qty.	Materials	Dimensions
A	Sides	4	1×12 pine	14" long
B	Bottom	1	1×12 pine	9¾" long
C	Long Trims	2	¾"-wide rope molding	12¾" long
D	Short Trims	2	¾"-wide rope molding	11¼" long

CONSTRUCTING THE WASTEBASKET

1. Cut four Sides (A) from 1×12 pine, each measuring 14 inches.

2. Place two Sides (A) on a level surface, parallel to each other and 9¾ inches apart. Apply glue to the meeting surfaces, and place a third Side (A) over the edges of the first two Sides (A), as shown in figure 1. Nail through the third Side (A) into the edges of the first two Sides (A). Use four 1½-inch nails evenly spaced along each joint.

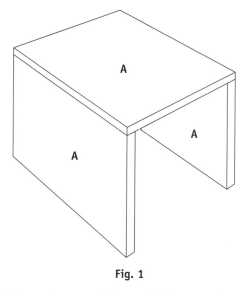

Fig. 1

3. Turn the assembly upside down and repeat step 2 to attach the fourth Side (A) to the assembly.

4. Cut one Bottom (B) from 1×12 pine, measuring 9¾ inches.

5. Fit the Bottom (B) inside the assembled Sides (A), flush with the ends of the Sides (A), as shown in figure 2. Apply glue to the meeting surfaces, and nail through the face of the four Sides (A) into the edge of the Bottom (B), using 1½-inch nails on each Side (A).

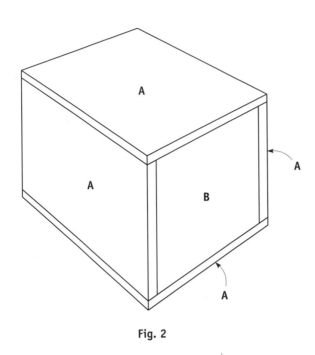

Fig. 2

Fig. 3

ADDING THE TOP TRIM

1. Cut two Long Trims (C) from ¾-inch-wide rope molding, each measuring 12¾ inches. Miter each end at opposing 45° angles.

2. Place the Sides/Bottom assembly so that the Bottom (B) is down on the working surface. Place the Long Trims (C) on the 12¾-inch top edge of the Sides (A), as shown in figure 3. Apply glue to the meeting surfaces, and nail through the Long Trims (C) into the edge of the Sides (A), using four 1-inch nails.

3. Cut two Short Trims (D) from ¾-inch-wide rope molding, each measuring 11¼ inches. Miter each end at opposing 45° angles.

4. Place the Short Trims (D) on the 11¼-inch top edge of the Sides (A), as shown in figure 3. Apply glue to the meeting surfaces, and nail through the Short Trims (D) into the edge of the Sides (A), using four 1-inch nails.

ADDING THE FEET

1. Place the assembled Sides/Bottom upside down so that the trims are on the working surface.

2. Using figure 4 as a guide, mark the holes for the foot screws. Drill holes through the Bottom (B) large enough to accommodate the drawer pull screws. Place the screws through the drilled

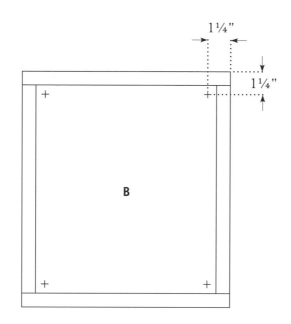

Fig. 4

holes from inside the assembly Bottom (B) and screw onto the round drawer pulls.

FINISHING THE WASTEBASKET

1. Fill any holes, cracks, or crevices with wood filler.

2. Thoroughly sand all areas of the completed wastebasket.

3. Paint or stain the wastebasket with the color of your choice. We chose a honey maple stain. We purchased a decorative stamp and gold paint, then stamped random designs over the stained wastebasket. See page 24 for more information on decorative painting.

Wooden Window Valance

Looking for unique and easy-to-make window treatments? This valance can be adjusted to fit any window, or painted to coordinate with your new or existing curtains. We added some sponge-painted trim to create extra visual interest.

MATERIALS

7 linear feet of 1×12 pine

7 linear feet of 1×4 pine

HARDWARE

30 1½" (4d) finish nails

4 metal shelf brackets

CUTTING LIST

Code	Description	Qty.	Materials	Dimensions
A	Front	1	1×12 pine	74¾" long
B	Sides	2	1×12 pine	2¾" long
C	Top	1	1×4 pine	74¾" long

Note: This valance can be adjusted to fit any window, by either subtracting or adding 5¾-inch cutout squares. Keep in mind, however, that to make the valance look symmetrical, you must always have an even number of cutouts. An alternate method is to change the width of the cutouts.

CUTTING THE PIECES

1. Cut one Front (A) from 1×12 plywood, measuring 74¾ inches.

2. Referring to figure 1, transfer the dimensions for the cutouts to the Front (A). To make certain that you cut out the properly sized squares, we suggest that you mark a large "X" on the areas to be cut out.

3. Cut out the squares marked with an "X" on the Front (A).

4. Cut two Sides (B) from 1×12 pine, each measuring 2¾ inches.

5. Cut one Top (C) from 1×4 pine, measuring 74¾ inches.

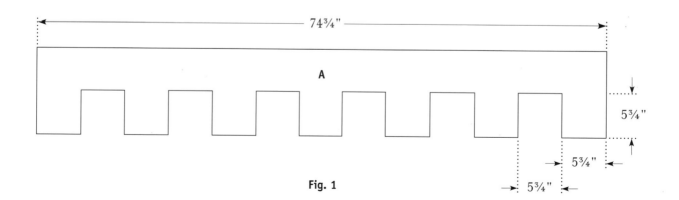

Fig. 1

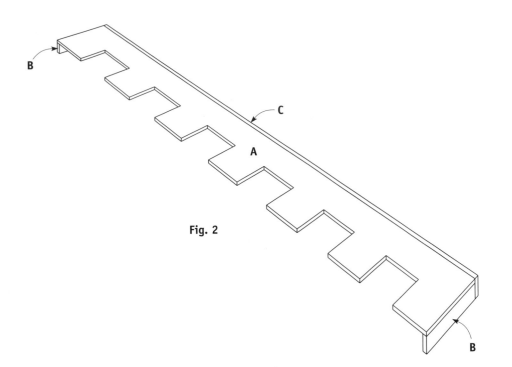

Fig. 2

ASSEMBLY

1. Place the two Sides (B) on end on a flat surface, parallel to each other, and 73½ inches apart. Apply glue to the meeting surfaces, and place the Front (A) over the ends of the Sides (B), as shown in figure 2. Nail through the Front (A) into the ends of the Sides (B), using four evenly spaced 1½-inch nails.

2. Stand the assembly upright and place the Top (C) over the edges of the Front (A) and Sides (B), as shown in figure 2. Apply glue to the meeting surfaces, and nail through the Top (C) into the edges of the Front (A) and Sides (B), using 1½-inch nails spaced every 5 inches.

FINISHING

1. Fill any holes, cracks, or crevices with wood filler.

2. Thoroughly sand all areas of the completed valance.

3. Paint or stain the valance with the color of your choice. We painted our valance pale green, then added sponged squares in a checkerboard pattern using pale pink paint.

4. Install four evenly spaced metal shelf brackets to the inside top of the valance. To hang, screw through the metal shelf brackets into the wall.

Faux Poster Bed

Although it looks as if it came from an expensive furniture store, it's really just a plywood headboard and footboard between four posts connected to an existing metal bed frame. Add ordinary curtain rods and holders, and voila—a charming four-poster bed!

MATERIALS

115 linear feet of 1×6 pine

6 linear feet of 1×8 pine

7 linear feet of 2×10 pine

2 4-×8-foot sheets of ¾" plywood

14 linear feet of 2¼" handrail

22 linear feet of 3"-wide beaded molding

8 3¾" decorative squares

7 linear feet of 1×4 pine

6 linear feet of 2×2 pine

2 closet rod holders

6 curtain rod holders

4 8-foot beaded curtain rods

6 curtain rod finials

HARDWARE

300 1½" (4d) finish nails

100 2" (6d) finish nails

60 1¼" (3d) finish nails

75 1" (2d) finish nails

20 2½" wood screws

20 1⅝" wood screws

CUTTING LIST

Code	Description	Qty.	Materials	Dimensions
A	Poster Side	16	1×6 pine	84" long
B	Small Base	8	1×8 pine	7¼" long
C	Large Base	8	2×10 pine	9¼" long
D	Headboard	1	¾" plywood	79"×34"
E	Top Rail	2	2¼" handrail	79" long
F	Long Molding	2	3"-wide beaded molding	57" long
G	Short Molding	2	3"-wide beaded molding	5" long
H	Decorative Squares	8	pine decorative squares	3¾" square
I	Footboard	1	¾" plywood	79"×28"
J	Long Footboard	2	3"-wide beaded molding	57" long
K	Short Footboard	2	3"-wide beaded molding	9½" long
L	Base Rail	1	1×4 pine	79" long
M	Supports	4	2×2 pine	15" long

MAKING THE POSTER COLUMNS

1. Cut 16 Poster Sides (A) from 1×6 pine, each measuring 84 inches.

2. Assemble four Poster Sides (A), overlapping each piece in rotation as shown in figure 1. With the four Sides (A) in position, the leg should measure 6¼ inches wide on all sides. Apply glue to the meeting surfaces, and nail together the four sides (A). Use 1½-inch nails, spacing nails about 6 inches apart.

3. Repeat step 2 three times to create the other three poster columns.

4. Cut eight Small Bases (B) from 1×8 pine, each measuring 7¼ inches.

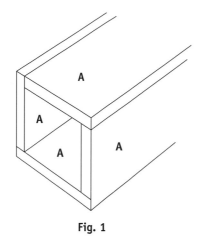

Fig. 1

5. Cut eight Large Bases (C) from 2×10 pine, each measuring 9¼ inches.

6. Center one Small Base (B) over one end of an assembled column, as shown in figure 2. Apply glue to the meeting surfaces, and nail through the Small Base (B) into the assembled column, using eight 1½-inch nails.

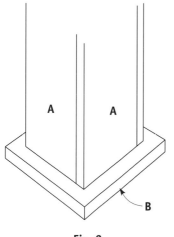

Fig. 2

7. Repeat step 6 to attach a second Small Base (B) to the opposite end of the same column.

8. Repeat steps 6 and 7 three times to attach the remaining seven Small Bases (B) on both ends of each of the remaining columns.

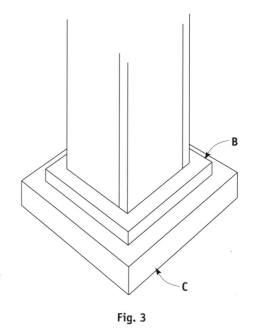

Fig. 3

9. Place one Large Base (C) on a flat, level surface (preferably the floor, due to the height of the columns). Center one assembled column with the Small Bases (B) attached, over the Large Base (C) as shown in figure 3. Apply glue to the meeting surfaces, and nail through the edge of the Small Base (B) into the Large Base (C), using eight 2-inch nails.

10. Turn the same column upside down, and repeat step 9 to attach a second Large Base (C).

11. Repeat steps 9 and 10 three times to attach the remaining Large Bases (C) to the ends of the remaining columns.

MAKING THE HEADBOARD

1. Cut one Headboard (D) from ¾-inch plywood, measuring 79×34 inches.

2. Cut two Top Rails (E) from 2¼-inch handrail, each measuring 79 inches.

3. Center one Top Rail (E) over the one 79-

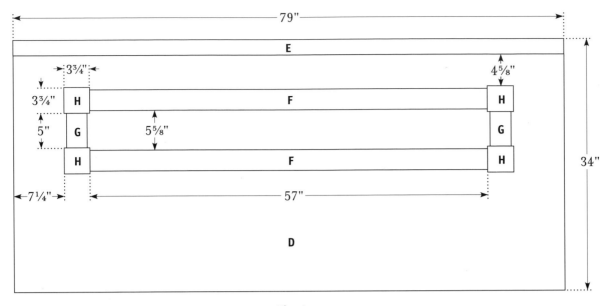

Fig. 4

inch edge of the Headboard (D). Apply glue to the meeting surfaces, and nail through the Top Rail (E) into the edge of the Headboard (D), using 2-inch nails spaced every 6 inches. Set the remaining Top Rail (E) aside; it will be used later on the footboard.

4. Cut two Long Moldings (F) from 3-inch-wide beaded molding, each measuring 57 inches.

5. Cut two Short Moldings (G) from 3-inch-wide beaded molding, each measuring 5 inches.

6. Referring to figure 4, position the Long and Short Moldings (F and G) and four Decorative Squares (H) on the Headboard (D). Note that the 3-inch moldings must be centered widthwise on the 3¾-inch Decorative Squares (H). Nail through each corner of the four Decorative Squares (H) using 1¼-inch nails. Nail through the molding, using 1-inch nails. Use two nails on each of the Short Moldings (G), and 11 nails on each of the Long Moldings (F).

MAKING THE FOOTBOARD

1. Cut one Footboard (I) from ¾-inch plywood, measuring 79×28 inches.

2. Locate the Top Rail (E) that you set aside earlier, and center the Top Rail (E) over the one 79-inch edge of the Footboard (I). Apply glue to the meeting surfaces, and nail through the Top Rail (E) into the edge of the Footboard (I), using 2-inch nails spaced every 6 inches.

3. Cut two Long Footboard Moldings (J) from 3-inch-wide beaded molding, each measuring 57 inches.

4. Cut two Short Footboard Moldings (K) from 3-inch-wide beaded molding, each measuring 9½ inches.

5. Referring to figure 5, position the Long and Short Footboard Moldings (J and K) and four Decorative Squares (H) on the Footboard (I). Note that the 3-inch moldings must be centered widthwise on the Decorative Squares (H). Nail through each corner of the four Decorative

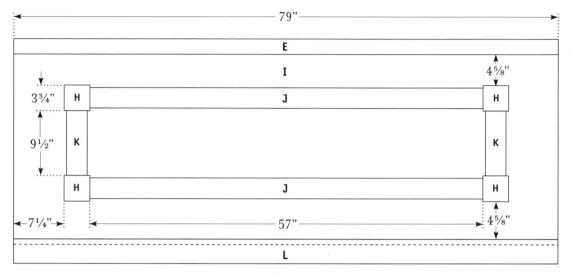

Fig. 5

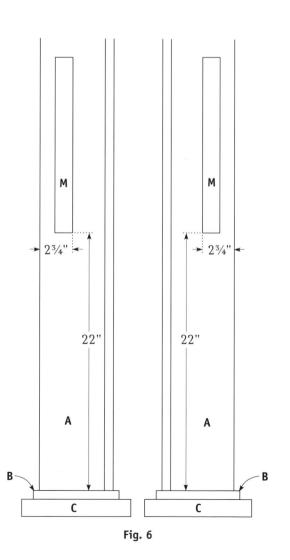

Fig. 6

Squares (H) using 1¼-inch nails. Nail through the molding, using 1-inch nails. Use two nails on each of the Short Footboard Moldings (K), and 11 nails on each of the Long Footboard Moldings (J).

6. Cut one Base Rail (L) from 1×4 pine, measuring 79 inches.

7. Apply glue to the meeting surfaces, and attach the Base Rail (L) to the bottom of the Footboard (I). The top of the Base Rail (L) should overlap the bottom of the Footboard (I) 1 inch. Use 1¼-inch nails spaced every 5 inches.

ASSEMBLING THE HEADBOARD AND FOOTBOARD

1. Cut four Supports (M) from 2×2 pine, each measuring 15 inches.

2. Attach two Supports (M) 22 inches above the bottom of two of the assembled columns into Side (A), as shown in figure 6. Apply glue to the meeting surfaces, and screw through the Support (M) into the Side (A), using four 2½-inch wood screws on each joint. (**Note:** These two columns will support the headboard.)

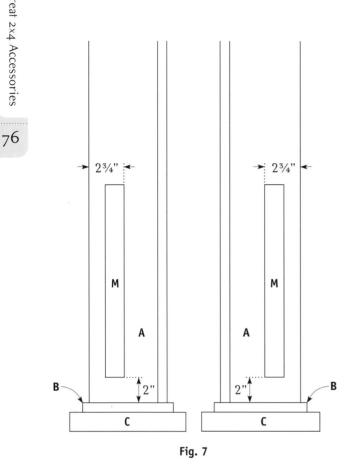

Fig. 7

3. Attach two Supports (M) 2 inches above the bottom of the remaining assembled columns, as shown in figure 7. Apply glue to the meeting surfaces, and screw through the Support (M) into the Side (A), using four 2½-inch wood screws. (**Note:** These two columns will support the footboard.)

4. Place the two headboard columns on a flat surface, with the two attached Supports (M) facing each other. Place the Headboard (D) over the two Supports (M) between the two headboard columns. The bottom of the Rail (L) should be flush against the top of the

Supports (M). Screw through the Headboard (D) into the Supports (M), using four 1⅝-inch wood screws on each joint.

5. Repeat step 4 to attach the footboard to the footboard columns.

FINISHING

1. Fill any holes, cracks, or crevices with wood filler.

2. Thoroughly sand all areas of the completed headboard and footboard assemblies.

3. Attach two closet rod holders on the inner sides of the two headboard columns, centered widthwise and 1½ inches from the top of the column.

4. Attach one curtain rod holder on the outside of each of the headboard columns.

5. Attach one curtain rod holder on the two outer sides of each of the footboard columns.

6. Paint or stain the project the color of your choice. We painted the entire bed assembly white. After the white paint dried, we applied a coat of light moss green paint, then ragged off

the second coat. Remember to paint the curtain rods and the finials. The curtain rods will be cut to length during the final assembly.

7. Depending on the type of metal frame on your bed, the installation of the headboard and footboard may vary. We had a metal frame with brackets for both a headboard and footboard, and screwed through the metal brackets into both the headboard and footboard. If your frame has only one bracket, you can turn the frame around and attach that bracket to the footboard. Then you can either attach the headboard to the wall or simply place the headboard against the wall and push the bed against it to hold it in place (assuming your bed is in no danger of moving across the floor).

8. Cut one beaded curtain rod to a length of 79 inches. Install the rod in the curtain rod holders above the headboard.

9. Screw a finial on one of the remaining curtain rods. Place the end with the finial on the curtain rod holder on the headboard column, and the other end on the curtain rod holder on the footboard column. Mark the desired length on the rod (ours extended past the holder about 1 inch), remove the curtain rod, and cut the rod at the mark. Screw a second finial into the cut end, and reinstall the curtain rod.

10. Repeat step 9 to install another curtain rod on the opposite side of the headboard/footboard.

11. Repeat the procedure one more time to cut and install the remaining curtain rod on the curtain rod holders over the footboard.

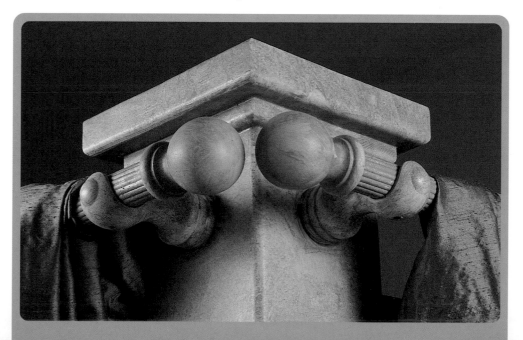

Birdhouse Floor Lamp

Place this cheerful floor lamp beside a comfortable chair in a corner of any room, and it will surely become your favorite spot to curl up with a good book. It's also a terrific addition to a garden room or a little girl's bedroom.

MATERIALS

18 linear feet of 1×8 pine

10 linear feet of 1×1 pine

4 linear feet of 2×4 pine

HARDWARE

50 1½" (4d) finish nails

30 1¼" (3d) finish nails

20 2½" (8d) finish nails

Lamp kit (available at most hardware stores)

Lamp shade of your choice

SPECIAL TOOLS & TECHNIQUES

Miter

Bar clamps

CUTTING LIST

Code	Description	Qty.	Materials	Dimensions
A	Back/Front	2	1×8 pine	46¼" long
B	Side	2	1×8 pine	43⅝" long
C	Roof	2	1×8 pine	10½" long
D	Side Trim	8	1×1 pine	8¾" long
E	Front Trim	4	1×1 pine	8¾" long
F	Base	4	2×4 pine	10½" long

CONSTRUCTING THE BASE

1. Cut two Back/Front pieces (A) from 1×8 pine, each measuring 46¼ inches.

2. Referring to figure 1, remove the shaded area on one end of a Back/Front (A).

3. Repeat step 2 to remove the shaded area on one end of the remaining Back/Front (A).

4. Cut two Sides (B) from 1×8 pine, each measuring 43⅛ inches.

5. Place the two Sides (B) on a level surface, parallel to each other and 5¾ inches apart. Apply glue to the meeting edges, and place one Back/Front (A) over the two Sides (B), as shown in figure 2 (page 80). Note that the square end of the Back/Front (A) is even with the ends of the Sides (B), and that the pointed end of the Back/Front (A) extends beyond the Sides (B). Nail through the Back/Front (A) into the edges of the two Sides (B), using 1½-inch nails spaced approximately every 5 inches.

6. Turn the assembly upside down, and repeat step 4 to attach the remaining Back/Front (A).

CONSTRUCTING THE ROOF

1. Cut two Roofs (C) from 1×8 pine, each measuring 10½ inches.

2. Bevel one 10½-inch edge of one Roof (C) at a 45° angle, as shown in figure 3.

3. Repeat step 2 to bevel one edge of the remaining Roof (C).

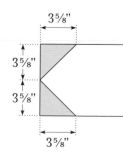

3⅝"

3⅝"

3⅝"

3⅝"

A

Fig. 1

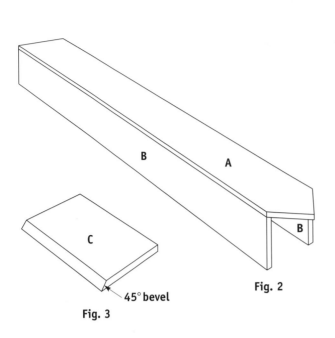

Fig. 2

Fig. 3

45° bevel

ADDING THE TRIM

1. Referring to figure 4, mark the trim placement lines on the two Sides (B) and one Back/Front(A) with a soft pencil.

2. Cut eight Side Trims (D) from 1×1 pine, each measuring 8¾ inches.

3. Apply glue to the meeting surfaces, and place one Side Trim (D) on the base assembly, under the penciled placement line. Nail through the Side Trim (D) into the Side (B), using two 1¼-inch nails.

4. Repeat step 3 seven times to attach the remaining Side Trims (D) to the base assembly.

5. Cut four Front Trims (E) from 1×1 pine, each measuring 8¾ inches.

6. Apply glue to the meeting surfaces, and attach one Front Trim (E) to the front of the base assembly (choose the best-looking peaked Back/Front [A]), under the placement line, and over the ends of the Side Trims (D). Nail through the Front Trim (E) into the Back/Front (A) and Side Trims (D), using three 1¼-inch nails.

7. Repeat step 6 three times to attach the remaining three Front Trims (E) to the front of the base assembly.

4. Apply glue to the beveled edges, and place the two Roofs (C), beveled edges together, on top of the base assembly, and nail pieces together. Nail through each of the Roofs (C) into the beveled edge of the other Roof (C), using four 1½-inch nails on each side. Do not nail into the base structure yet, as the roof will have to be removed to wire the lamp.

5. Drill a ½-inch-diameter hole through the center of the roof peak to accommodate the later addition of the lamp parts.

6. Remove the completed roof, and set it aside.

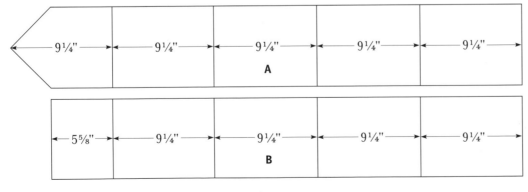

Fig. 4

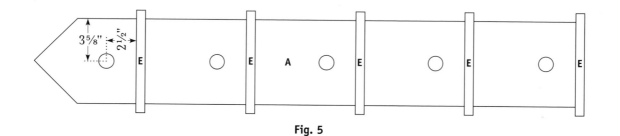

Fig. 5

COMPLETING THE BASE ASSEMBLY

1. Referring to figure 5, mark the placement of five holes in the front of the base assembly.

2. Drill five 1¼-inch-diameter holes through the front of the base assembly, using the marks as a guide.

3. Cut four Bases (F) from 2×4 pine, each measuring 10½ inches.

4. Miter the ends of each of the four Bases (F) at opposing 45° angles, as shown in figure 6.

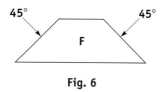

Fig. 6

5. Apply glue to the meeting surfaces, and position the four Bases (F), with the mitered ends together, to form a square, as shown in figure 7.

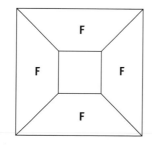

Fig. 7

6. Clamp the four Bases (F) together, and toenail through both sides of each joint to hold the assembly together. Use two 2½-inch nails on each joint.

7. Center the four Bases (F) over the bottom of the base assembly. Nail through the Bases (F) into the bottom edges of the two Back/Fronts (A) and the two Sides (B). Use two 2½-inch nails through each Base (F).

FINISHING

1. Fill all cracks and crevices with wood filler.

2. Sand the completed floor lamp thoroughly.

3. Paint the floor lamp the color of your choice. We painted the roof and the trim hunter green, and the rest of the lamp bright white.

4. Install the lamp kit following the manufacturer's instructions.

5. Center the assembled roof (with lamp kit installed) over the top of the base assembly, threading the wire through the center of the assembly. Apply glue to the meeting surfaces, and nail through each side of the roof into the Back/Fronts (A) and the Sides (B). Use two 1½-inch nails on each of the roof sections.

Breakfast Tray

If you're a pushover for lazy weekend mornings in bed, you'll love this generously sized breakfast tray. It's large enough for a newspaper, a pot of coffee, and a plate of delectable goodies.

MATERIALS

2-×4-foot sheet of ¾" plywood

7 linear feet of 1×3 pine

1 linear feet of ¾"-wide rope molding

HARDWARE

20 2" finish nails

6 1⅝" wood screws

4 1" finish nails

CUTTING LIST

Code	Description	Qty.	Materials	Dimensions
A	Tray Stands	2	¾" plywood	12"×13"
B	Tray Top	1	¾" plywood	24"×13"
C	Long Tray Sides	2	1×3 pine	24" long
D	Short Tray Sides	2	1×3 pine	14½" long
E	Stand Trims	4	¾"-wide rope molding	11¼" long

MAKING THE TRAY

1. Cut two Tray Stands (A) from ¾" plywood, each measuring 12×13 inches.

2. Cut one Tray Top (B) from ¾" plywood, measuring 24×13 inches.

3. Using figure 1 as a guide, place the two Tray Stands (A) on edge 22½ inches apart with the 13-inch edge at the top. Place the Tray Top (B) over the ends of the Tray Stands (A). Apply glue to the meeting surfaces, and nail through the face of the Tray Top (B) into the edges of the Tray Stands (A) using four 2-inch nails.

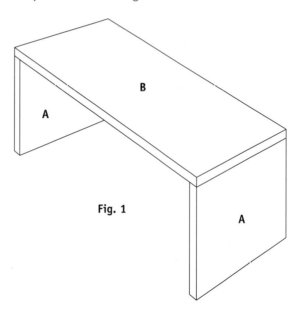

Fig. 1

4. Cut two Long Tray Sides (C) from 1×3 pine, each measuring 24 inches.

5. Place the Long Tray Sides (C) over the 24-inch edges of the Tray Top (B). The Long Tray Sides (C) will extend 1 inch above and ¾ inch below the Tray Top (B), as shown in figure 2. Apply glue to the meeting surfaces, and nail through the Long Tray Sides (C) into the edge

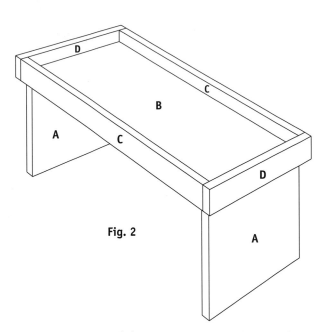

Fig. 2

of the Tray Top (B), using 2-inch nails spaced 5 inches apart.

6. Cut two Short Tray Sides (D) from 1×3 pine, each measuring 14½ inches.

7. Place the two Short Tray Sides (D) over the ends of the Tray Top (B), as shown in figure 2. Apply glue to the meeting surfaces, and nail through the Short Tray Sides (D) into the edges of the Tray Top (B) using four 2-inch nails.

8. Using three 1⅝-inch screws on each side, screw through the Short Tray Sides (D) into the Tray Stands (A). This will give added support to the Tray Stands (A).

ADDING THE TRIM

1. Cut four Stand Trims (E) from ¾-inch-wide rope molding, each measuring 11¼ inches.

2. Place the Stand Trims (E) over the exposed plywood edges of the Tray Stands (A). Apply glue to the meeting surfaces. Nail through the Stand Trims (E) into the Tray Stands (A) using four 1-inch nails.

FINISHING

1. Fill all cracks, crevices, and nail holes with wood filler.

2. Thoroughly sand the completed breakfast tray.

3. Paint or stain the tray the color of your choice.

4. After our paint dried, we added a little whimsy to our breakfast tray. We went to a color copy store and copied a plate, butter knife, napkin, and cup and saucer; then we cut out the copies and decoupaged newsprint and the color copies to the top of the tray. The finished project was then sealed with a coat of polyurethane.

Kitchen Island Topper

We love this great island topper. It keeps everyday china accessible—plates for sandwiches or bowls for morning cereal—and it frees up lots of kitchen cabinet space.

MATERIALS

8 linear feet of 1×1 pine

22 linear feet of ⅜"-diameter wooden dowel rod

12 linear feet of 1×10 pine

5 linear feet of 2×2 pine

9 linear feet of 1×12 pine

8 linear feet of ¾"-wide cove molding

HARDWARE

30 1⅝" wood screws

20 1¼" (3d) finish nails

50 1" (2d) finish nails

SPECIAL TOOLS & TECHNIQUES

Router and a round-over bit (optional)

Bar clamps

Miter

CUTTING LIST

Code	Description	Qty.	Materials	Dimensions
A	Rack Support	4	1×1 pine	22½" long
B	Rack Rod	18	⅜" dia. dowel	14" long
C	Inner Vertical	2	1×10 pine	14" long
D	Shelf	2	1×10 pine	11¾" long
E	Shelf Support	4	2×2 pine	14" long
F	Inner Top/Bottom	2	1×10 pine	47½" long
G	Top/Bottom	2	1×12 pine	49½" long
H	Cove Molding	8	¾"-wide cove molding	cut to fit

MAKING THE PLATE RACK

1. Cut four Rack Supports (A) from 1×1 pine, each measuring 22½ inches.

2. Holes must be drilled in each of the four Rack Supports (A) to accommodate the dowel rods that hold the plates. It is very important that the holes are accurate and straight, or your finished plate rack will be crooked. Referring to the measurements in figure 1, drill nine ⅜-inch-diameter holes in one Rack Support (A). Note that the holes are centered widthwise on the Rack Support (A), and 2¼ inches apart on center.

3. Use the drilled Rack Support (A) as a template to drill holes in each of the remaining three Rack Supports (A).

4. Cut 18 Rack Rods (B) from ⅜-inch-diameter dowel rod, each measuring 14 inches.

5. Place one Rack Support (A), with the holes facing up, on a flat surface. Apply glue to the end of one Rack Rod (B), and insert it in the first hole in the Rack Support (A). Make certain that the Rack Rod (B) is completely through the hole and flush with the bottom surface of the Rack Support (A).

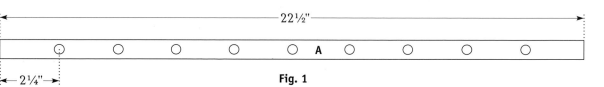

22½"

2¼"

Fig. 1

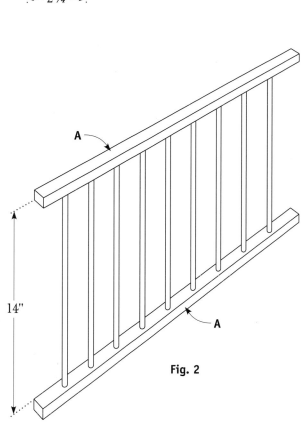

A

14"

A

Fig. 2

6. Repeat step 5 eight times to insert eight additional Rack Rods (B) in the first Rack Support (A). Let the glue set up for several hours.

7. Place a second Rack Support (A) on a level surface. Turn the Rack Rod/Support assembly upside down, apply glue to the exposed ends of each of the Rack Rods (B), and insert each Rack Rod (B) into the corresponding holes in the second Rack Support (A) to form a ladder arrangement, as shown in figure 2.

8. Repeat steps 5 through 7 to assemble the second rack assembly, using the remaining nine Rack Rods (B), and remaining two Rack Supports (A).

ASSEMBLING THE SHELF SECTIONS

1. Cut two Inner Verticals (C) from 1×10 pine, each measuring 14 inches.

2. Cut two Shelves (D) from 1×10 pine, each measuring 11¾ inches.

3. Cut four Shelf Supports (E) from 2×2 pine, each measuring 14 inches.

4. An optional step is to cut two ⅛-×⅛-inch grooves on all four sides of each Shelf Support (E). (This is for decorative purposes only.)

5. Place one Shelf (D) on a flat surface. Referring to figure 3, mark the cutout to accommodate a Shelf Support (E) in the two outer corners of the Shelf (D). Place the end of one Shelf Support (E) exactly in place, and trace around it. Remove the Shelf Support (E), and cut out the marked corners from the Shelf (D).

6. Repeat step 5 to cut out the corners on the remaining Shelf (D).

7. Place one Inner Vertical (C) on edge on a flat surface. Center the Shelf (D) over the Inner Vertical (C), with the cutouts facing up, as shown in figure 4. Apply glue to the meeting surfaces and screw through the Inner Vertical (C) into the edge of the Shelf (D), using four 1⅝-inch wood screws.

CUTTING THE TOP/BOTTOMS

1. Cut two Inner Top/Bottoms (F) from 1×10 pine, each measuring 47½ inches.

2. Cut two Top/Bottoms (G) from 1×12 pine, each measuring 49½ inches.

3. An optional step at this point is to use a router and a round-over bit to finish the edges of each of the two Top/Bottoms (G).

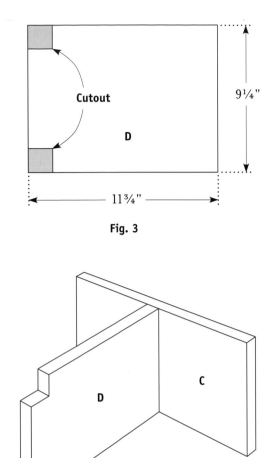

Cutout

D

9¼"

11¾"

Fig. 3

D

C

Fig. 4

ASSEMBLY

1. Place the two Inner Top/Bottoms (F) on edge on a level surface, parallel to each other and 14 inches apart. Fit one rack/rod assembly (centered lengthwise) between the two Inner Top/Bottoms (F), as shown in figure 5. Place one shelf assembly on each end of the centered rack/rod assembly. Apply glue to the meeting surfaces, clamp the assembly together to hold it in position, and screw through the Inner Verticals (C) into the ends of the rack/rod assemblies, using a 1⅝-inch screw on each joint.

2. Apply glue on the meeting surfaces, and screw through the Inner Top/Bottoms (F) into the edge of each Inner Vertical (C), using three 1⅝-inch screws on each joint.

3. Apply glue to the meeting surfaces, and fit the Shelf Supports (E) between the Inner Top/Bottoms (F), and into the cut-out corners of the Shelves (D). Screw through the Inner Top/Bottoms (F) into the ends of each Shelf Support (E), using a 1⅝-inch screw on each joint.

4. Apply glue to the meeting surfaces, and center one Top/Bottom (G) on one Inner Top/Bottom (F). There should be a 1-inch-wide overhang on all sides. Nail through the Top/Bottom (G) into the Inner Top/Bottom (F) using 1¼-inch nails. Use three nails on each end, and about five nails along each side.

5. Turn the assembly upside down, and repeat step 4 to attach the remaining Top/Bottom (G) to the remaining Inner Top/Bottom (F).

6. Miter cut and fit ¾-inch Cove Molding (H) over the joining of the

lower Inner Top/Bottom (F) and the lower Top/Bottom (G). Apply glue to the meeting surfaces, and nail through the cove molding into the Top/Bottom (G) using 1-inch nails spaced about every 4 inches.

7. Turn the assembly upside down and repeat step 6 to attach Cove Molding (H) to the joining of the remaining Inner Top/Bottom (F) and Top/Bottom (G).

FINISHING

1. Fill any holes, cracks, or crevices with wood filler.

2. Thoroughly sand all areas of the completed island topper.

3. Paint or stain the island topper with the color of your choice. We chose a very light pine stain, then sealed the topper with a satin polyurethane.

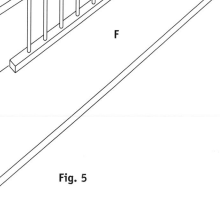

Fig. 5

Wine Cabinet

Our wine rack doubles as a serving bar; it has storage for bottles below, and accommodates lots of glasses above. The bottom opens for extra storage, and the tile surface serves as an instant bar, saving those constant treks to the kitchen for mixing drinks.

MATERIALS

2 4-×8-foot sheets of ¾" plywood

42 linear feet of 1×4 pine

1 4-×4-foot sheet of ⅜" plywood

22 linear feet of 1×3 pine

5 linear feet of 1×1 pine

8 linear feet of 3¼"-wide crown molding

8 linear feet of ¾"-wide cove molding

Ceramic tile, enough to cover 3½ square feet

Small container of ceramic tile adhesive

7-lb. bag of sanded tile grout in the color of your choice

Grout sealer

HARDWARE

120 1⅝" wood screws

6 1½" (4d) finish nails

55 1" drywall screws

15 1¼" drywall screws

30 1" (2d) finish nails

8 cabinet door hinges

4 magnetic door catches

4 drawer pulls

SPECIAL TOOLS & TECHNIQUES

Bar clamps

Miters

Trowel (for applying tile adhesive)

Rubber tile float

CUTTING LIST

Code	Description	Qty.	Materials	Dimensions
A	Side	2	¾" plywood	63¼"×15¼"
B	Top/Bottom	2	¾" plywood	33⅜"×15¼"
C	Shelf	3	¾" plywood	31⅞"×15¼"
D	Vertical Trim	2	1×4 pine	64¾" long
E	Horizontal Trim	3	1×4 pine	26⅜" long
F	Horizontal Wine Trim	2	1×4 pine	26⅜" long
G	Ledge	1	1×4 pine	31⅞" long
H	Upper Panel	2	⅜" plywood	19¾"×11⅜"
I	Upper Vertical Trim	4	1×3 pine	21¾" long
J	Upper Horizontal Trim	4	1×3 pine	8¾" long
K	Lower Panel	2	⅜" plywood	15¼"×11⅜"
L	Lower Vertical Trim	4	1×3 pine	17¼" long
M	Lower Horizontal Trim	4	1×3 pine	8¾" long
N	Wine Bottle Support	2	1×4 pine	31⅞" long
O	Side Base Support	2	1×4 pine	17⅝" long
P	Front Base Support	1	1×4 pine	35¼" long
Q	Stem Supports	5	1×4 pine	10" long
R	Connectors	5	1×1 pine	10" long
S	Frame Supports	2	1×4 pine	31" long
T	Top Molding		3¼"-wide crown molding	cut to fit
U	Base Molding		¾"-wide crown molding	cut to fit

*Notes on Materials

Most tiles sold at building-supply stores are now "self-spacing"; that is, they come with small projections on their edges so that when you lay the tiles out, the grout lines between them will be even. Because the spacing is determined by individual tile manufacturers, we recommend that you buy enough tile to cover the square foot area specified. If the tiles do not fit exactly, you will also need to purchase a tile cutter to cut the necessary tiles at the back and one side of the shelf.

CONSTRUCTING THE CABINET

1. Cut two Sides (A) from ¾-inch plywood, each measuring 63¼×15¼ inches.

2. Cut two Top/Bottoms (B) from ¾-inch plywood, each measuring 33⅜×15¼ inches.

3. Place the two Sides (A) on edge on a level surface parallel to each other 31⅞ inches apart. Fit the Top/Bottoms (B) over the ends of the Sides (A) to form a rectangle measuring 64¾×33⅜ inches, as shown in figure 1. Apply glue to the meeting surfaces, and screw through the Top/Bottoms (B) into the edge of the Sides (A). Use 1⅝-inch wood screws spaced about every 5 inches.

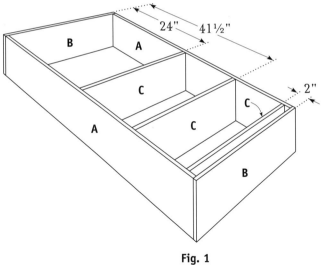

Fig. 1

4. Cut three Shelves (C) from ¾-inch plywood, each measuring 31⅞×15¼ inches. Place the first Shelf (C) 24 inches below the Top (B), as shown in figure 1. Screw through the Sides (A) into the edges of the Shelf (C). Use 1⅝-inch wood screws spaced every 5 inches.

5. Repeat step 4 to attach the second Shelf (C) 41½ inches below the Top (B).

6. Repeat step 4 to attach the third Shelf (C) 2 inches above the Bottom (B).

ADDING THE FRONT TRIM AND LEDGE

1. Cut two Vertical Trims (D) from 1×4 pine, each measuring 64¾ inches. Apply glue to the meeting surfaces, and place one Vertical Trim (D) over the edge of one Side (A). Screw through the Vertical Trim (D) into the edge of Side (A), as shown in figure 2. Use 1⅝-inch wood screws about every 5 inches.

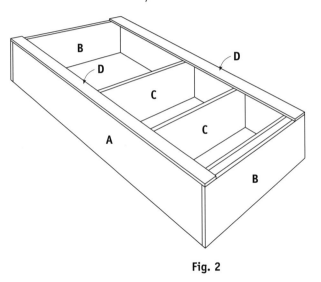

Fig. 2

2. Repeat step 1 to attach the remaining Vertical Trim (D) to the opposing Side (A).

3. Cut three Horizontal Trims (E) from 1×4 pine, each measuring 26⅜ inches.

4. Apply glue to the meeting surfaces, and attach one Horizontal Trim (E) over the edge of the Top (B), as shown in figure 3. Screw through the Horizontal Trim (E) into the edge of the Top (B). Use 1⅝-inch wood screws spaced every 5 inches.

5. Repeat step 4 to attach the remaining two Horizontal Trims (E) flush with the upper edge

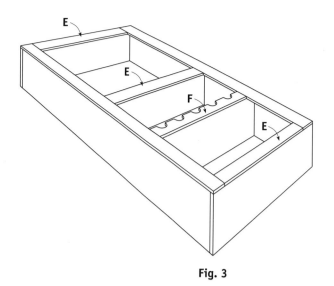

Fig. 3

of the Shelf (C) and flush with the lower edge of the Bottom (B). See figure 3.

6. Cut two Horizontal Wine Trims (F) from 1×4 pine, each measuring 26⅜ inches.

7. Referring to figure 4, mark and cut the semi-circular cuts that will hold the tops of the wine bottles. Apply glue to the meeting surfaces, and attach one of the Horizontal Wine Trims (F) on the edge of the lower Shelf (C), as shown in figure 3. Use 1⅝-inch wood screws spaced every 5 inches.

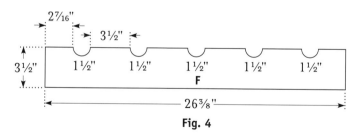

Fig. 4

8. Repeat step 7 to attach the second Horizontal Wine Trim (F) 5½ inches above the first Horizontal Wine Trim (F). Apply glue to the meeting surfaces, and fit the second Horizontal Wine Trim (F) between the two Vertical Trims (D). Toenail through the Horizontal Wine Trim (F) into each of the Vertical Trims (D). Use 1½-inch nails.

9. Cut one Ledge (G) from 1×4 pine, measuring 31⅞ inches. Place the Ledge (G) between the two Sides (A) 18½ inches below the Top (B), as shown in figure 5. Use 1⅝-inch wood screws to attach.

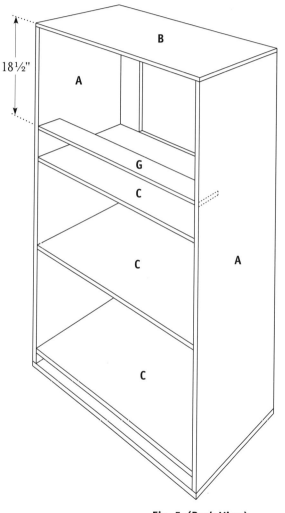

Fig. 5 (Back View)

MAKING THE DOOR PANELS

1. Cut two Upper Panels (H) from ⅜-inch plywood, each measuring 19¾×11⅜ inches.

2. Cut four Upper Vertical Trims (I) for the door from 1×3 pine, each measuring 21¾ inches.

3. Cut four Upper Horizontal Trims (J) for the door from 1×3 pine, each measuring 8¾ inches.

4. Position two of the Upper Vertical Trims (I) face down on a level surface, parallel to each other and 8¾ inches apart. Position two of the Upper Horizontal Trims (J) between the Upper Vertical Trims (I), as shown in figure 6. Apply glue to the meeting surfaces. Hold the trims in place temporarily using bar clamps.

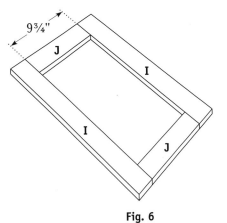

Fig. 6

5. Center one Upper Panel (H) over the Trims (I and J), as shown in figure 7. Apply glue to the meeting surfaces, and screw through the Upper Panel (H) into Horizontal and Vertical Trims (I and J) using 1-inch drywall screws spaced every 5 inches.

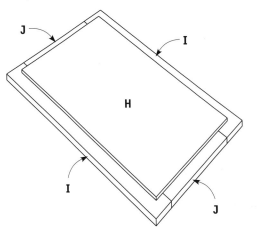

Fig. 7

6. Repeat steps 4 and 5 to create the second door panel.

7. Cut two Lower Panels (K) for the door from ⅜-inch plywood, each measuring 15¼×11⅜.

8. Cut four Lower Vertical Trims (L) for the door from 1×3 pine, each measuring 17¼ inches.

9. Cut four Lower Horizontal Trims (M) for the door from 1×3 pine, each measuring 8¾ inches.

10. Position two of the Lower Vertical Trims (L) face down on a level surface parallel to each other and 8¾ inches apart. Position two of the Lower Horizontal Trims (M) between the Lower Vertical Trims (L) 12¼ inches apart, as you did for the Upper Trims (I and J) (see figure 6). Apply glue to the meeting surfaces, and use bar clamps to hold the Horizontal and Vertical Trims (L and M) in place temporarily.

11. Center one Lower Panel (K) face down over the Lower Trims (L and M), as you did for the Upper Trims (I and J) (see figure 7). Apply glue to the meeting surfaces, and screw through the edges of the Lower Panel (K) into the Lower Vertical and Horizontal Trims (L and M), using 1-inch drywall screws spaced every 5 inches.

12. Repeat steps 10 and 11 to construct another lower door.

ADDING THE BOTTLE SUPPORTS

1. Cut two Wine Bottle Supports (N) from 1×4 pine, each measuring 31⅞ inches. Referring to figure 8, cut five semicircular cutouts to hold

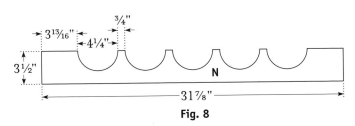

Fig. 8

the bottom of the wine bottles. Each cutout has a radius of 4¼ inches. (The cutout is the same diameter as one-quarter of a paint can.) Use 1⅝-inch wood screws to attach the Wine Bottle Supports (N) level with and 6 inches behind the Horizontal Wine Trims (F). Screw through the Sides (A) into the end of the Wine Bottle Supports (N), using two screws for each end.

2. Cut two Side Base Supports (O) from 1×4 pine, each measuring 17⅝ inches. Miter one end of each of the Side Base Supports (O) at a 45° angle, as shown in figure 9.

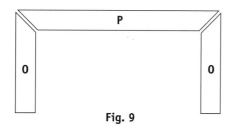

Fig. 9

3. Cut one Front Base Support (P) from 1×4 pine, measuring 35¼ inches. Miter the ends of the Front Base Support (P) at opposing 45° angles, as shown in figure 9.

4. Apply glue to the meeting surfaces, and attach the Base Supports (O and P) to the Bottom (B), as shown in figure 10. Use 1⅝-inch wood screws spaced 5 inches apart.

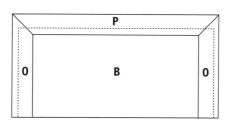

Fig. 10

ADDING THE GLASS HOLDERS

1. Cut five Stem Supports (Q) from 1×4 pine, each measuring 10 inches.

2. Cut five Connectors (R) from 1×1 pine, each measuring 10 inches.

3. Cut two Frame Supports (S) from 1×4 pine, each measuring 31 inches.

4. Apply glue to the meeting surfaces and center one Connector (R) lengthwise over one Stem Support (Q), as shown in figure 11. Nail through the Connector (R) into the Stem Support (Q), using four evenly spaced 1⅝-inch wood screws.

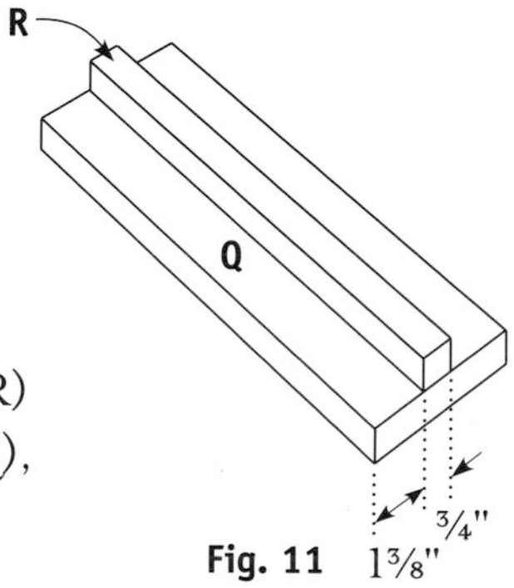

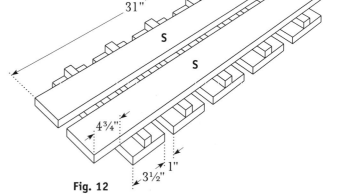

Fig. 11

5. Repeat step 4 four times to attach the remaining Connectors (R) to the remaining Stem Supports (Q).

6. Place the five connector/support assemblies on a level surface, parallel to each other and 1 inch apart. Center the two Frame Supports (S) over the five connector/support assemblies as shown in figure 12. Note that the Frame Supports (S) will overhang the connector/support assemblies by 4¾ inches on each side.

Fig. 12

7. Center the entire glass holder assembly inside the cabinet under the Top (B), flush with the back edge of the cabinet. Apply glue to the meeting surfaces and screw through the two Frame Supports (S) into the Top (B). Use 1¼-inch drywall screws spaced 5 inches apart.

INSTALLING THE DOORS

1. Place the completed cabinet on its back, and fit the four cabinet doors over the front openings in the cabinet. Allow about ⅛ inch between the doors. Check to make certain that the doors are level and fit evenly over the openings in the cabinet.

2. Attach the doors to the cabinet using two hinges on each door. Attach door catches on each of the doors to make certain that they stay closed when shut.

3. Install a drawer pull on each of the cabinets, following the manufacturer's instructions.

FINISHING

1. Stand the cabinet upright. Refer to the photograph when placing the molding. If you're not skilled at cutting molding, refer to page 23. Carefully cut 3¼-inch-wide crown molding (T) to fit around the top of the cabinet. Use glue and 1-inch (2d) finish nails spaced every 5 inches. The bottom of the crown molding (T) should overlap the top of the cabinet by ½ inch.

2. Cut ¾-inch-wide cove molding (U) to fit around the bottom of the cabinet. Use glue and 1-inch finish nails spaced every 5 inches.

3. Fill all nail and screw holes, cracks, and crevices with wood filler.

4. Sand all surfaces of the completed wine cabinet.

5. Stain or paint the cabinet with the color of your choice. We chose a cherry stain, then sealed it with a clear polyurethane.

ADDING THE TILE

1. The last step is to install the tile on the top shelf. Following the manufacturer's directions carefully, spread an even coat of tile adhesive over the surface of the top shelf with a trowel.

2. Place the tiles on the adhesive one at a time, making sure that the tiles are straight. Do not slide tiles, or the adhesive will be forced up onto the sides of the tiles. Let the adhesive dry overnight.

3. Mix the tile grout according to the manufacturer's directions (or use premixed tile grout).

4. Using a rubber-surfaced float, spread the grout over the tiles with arcing motions. Hold the float at an angle so that the grout is forced evenly into the spaces between the tiles.

5. When the grout begins to set up, use a damp rag to wipe the excess from the tiles and joints. If you let the grout harden too long, it will be very difficult to remove. Use as little water as possible when removing the excess so that you don't thin the grout that remains. Let the grout dry overnight.

6. Use a damp rag to wipe the remaining film from the tile.

7. Apply grout sealer, following the manufacturer's directions. (You may need to wait several days before applying sealer to the project.)

Scrap-Wood Candlesticks

This project makes use of the scrap wood that may be lurking in your workshop. We simply cut squares from wood scraps to 1¾-, 2½-, and 3-inch sizes, painted them, and nailed the pieces together. The candlesticks are assembled in different arrangements: a simple stack, a star, and two free-form candlesticks. Either replicate one of our designs or come up with your own.

MATERIALS

Assorted scrap wood cut into squares
(see cutting list below)

HARDWARE

20 1¼" (3d) finish nails (for all four candlesticks)

CUTTING LIST

Code	Description	Qty.	Materials	Dimensions
A	Stack (Small)	1	1" pine	1¾" square
B	Stack (Medium)	1	1" pine	2½" square
C	Stack (Large)	1	1" pine	3" square
D	Star (Small)	1	1" pine	1¾" square
E	Star (Medium)	2	1" pine	2½" square
F	Star (Large)	1	2" pine	3" square
G	Tall Free-Form (Small)	3	1" pine	1¾" square
H	Tall Free-Form (Medium)	2	1" pine	2½" square
I	Tall Free-Form (Large)	2	1" pine	3" square
J	Tall Free-Form (X-Large)	1	2" pine	3" square
K	Short Free-Form (Small)	2	1" pine	1¾" square
L	Short Free-Form (Medium)	3	1" pine	2½" square
M	Short Free-Form (Large)	3	1" pine	3" square

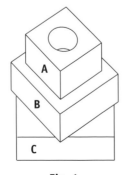

Fig. 1

MAKING THE SIMPLE STACK CANDLESTICK

1. Cut squares to the following measurements
from 1-inch-thick wood: one Small square
(A) measuring 1¾ inches square, one Medium
square (B) measuring 2½ inches square, and one
Large square (C) measuring 3 inches squares.

2. Sand and paint each of the pieces, and allow
them to dry thoroughly.

3. Refer to figure 1 during assembly. Place the
Large square (C) on a level surface. Center the
Medium square (B) over it at a 45° angle, and nail
the two pieces together using two 1¼-inch nails.

4. Drill a ¾-inch-diameter hole in the center of
the Small square (A) to accommodate the candle.

5. Center the Small square (A) over the assembly,
and nail through the drilled hole into the
assembly using two 1¼-inch nails.

MAKING THE STAR CANDLESTICK

1. Cut squares to the following measurements
from 1-inch-thick wood: one Small square (D)
measuring 1¾ inches, and two Medium squares
(E), measuring 2½ inches.

2. Cut one Large square (F) from 2-inch-thick
wood, measuring 3 inches.

3. Sand and paint each of the pieces, and allow
them to dry thoroughly.

4. Refer to figure 2 during assembly. Place the
Large square (F) on a level surface. Center
one Medium square (E) over it at a 45° angle,
and nail the two pieces together using two
1¼-inch nails.

5. Center the second Medium square (E) over
the assembly, again at a 45° angle, and nail the
two pieces together using two 1¼-inch nails.

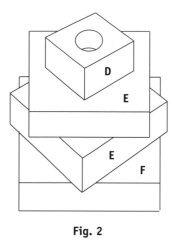

Fig. 2

6. Drill a ¾-inch-diameter hole in the center of the Small square (D) to accommodate the candle.

7. Center the Small square (D) over the assembly, and nail through the drilled hole into the assembly using two 1¼-inch nails.

MAKING THE TALL FREE-FORM CANDLESTICK

1. Cut squares to the following measurements from 1-inch-thick wood: three Small squares (G), each measuring 1¾ inches; two Medium squares (H), each measuring 2½ inches; and two Large squares (I), each measuring 3 inches.

2. Cut one Extra-Large square (J) from 2-inch-thick wood, measuring 3 inches.

3. Sand and paint each of the pieces, and allow them to dry thoroughly.

4. Refer to figure 3 during assembly. The assembly of the free-form requires two intermediate assembly processes. Place one Small square (G) on end on a level surface. Center one Large square (I) over the end of the Small square (G) at a 45° angle. Nail through the Large square (I) into the end of the Small square (G) using two 1¼-inch nails.

5. Turn the assembly over, and center one Medium square (H) over the end of the Small

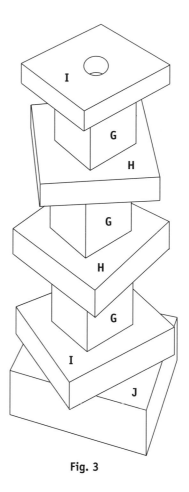

Fig. 3

square (G) at a 45° angle. Nail through the Medium square (H) into the Small square (G) using two 1¼-inch nails.

6. Drill a ¾-inch-diameter hole ½ inch deep in the center of one Large square (I).

7. Repeat steps 4 and 5 to complete a second intermediate assembly, making certain that the drilled hole on the Large square (I) ends up on the outside of the assembly.

8. Place the 2-inch-thick Extra-Large square (J) on a flat surface. Center the first intermediate assembly (without the drilled hole), Large square (I) down, at a 45° angle over the Extra-Large square (J). Nail through the edges of the Large square (I) into the Extra-Large square (J) using two 1¼-inch nails.

9. Center one Small square (G) over the assembly, again at a 45° angle, and nail through the Small square (G) into the Medium square (H) using two 1¼-inch nails.

10. Center the second intermediate assembly at a 45° angle over the Small square (G). Nail through the Medium square (H) into the Small square (G) using two 1¼-inch nails.

SHORT FREE-FORM CANDLESTICK

1. Cut squares to the following measurements from 1-inch-thick wood: two Small squares (K), each measuring 1¾ inches; three Medium squares (L), each measuring 2½ inches; and three Large squares (M), each measuring 3 inches.

2. Sand and paint each of the pieces, and allow them to dry thoroughly.

3. Refer to figure 4 during the assembly. The assembly of the short free-form requires two intermediate assembly processes. Place one Small square (K) on end on a level surface. Center one Large square (M) over the end of the Small square (K) at a 45° angle. Nail through the Large square (M) into the end of the Small square (K) using two 1¼-inch nails.

4. Turn the assembly over, and center one Medium square (L) over the end of the Small square (K) at a 45° angle. Nail through the medium square (L) into the Small square (K) using two 1¼-inch nails.

5. Repeat steps 3 and 4 to complete a second intermediate assembly, this time using one Small square (K) in the center, and two Medium squares (L) on the outside.

6. Place one Large square (M) on a flat surface. Center the first intermediate assembly (with the Large square [M] at the top), at a 45° angle over

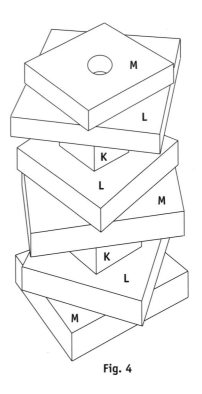

Fig. 4

the Large square (M). Nail through the edges of the Medium square (L) into the Large square (M) using two 1¼-inch nails.

7. Repeat step 6 to attach the second intermediate assembly.

8. Drill a ¾-inch-diameter hole in the center of the remaining Large square (M).

9. Center the Large square (M) (hole side up) over the assembly, again at a 45° angle, and nail through the drilled hole into the Medium square (L) using two 1¼-inch nails.

Plate Rack

This plate rack is a perfect place to display your collectible plates. Or hang it in a convenient spot on your kitchen wall and store your most frequently used dishes and cups.

MATERIALS

10 linear feet of 1×6 pine

5 linear feet of 1×4 pine

3 linear feet of 1×8 pine

10 linear feet of ⅜"-diameter dowel rod

HARDWARE

20 1⅝" wood screws

4 hanging hooks

SPECIAL TOOLS & TECHNIQUES

Clamps

CUTTING LIST

Code	Description	Qty.	Materials	Dimensions
A	Rack Sides	2	1×6 pine	26" long
B	Rack Top/Bottom	2	1×6 pine	24½" long
C	Rack Middle	1	1×4 pine	24½" long
D	Rack Ledge	1	1×8 pine	28" long
E	Rack Base	1	1×4 pine	24½" long
F	Dowel	4	⅜" dowel rod	25" long

MAKING THE RACK

1. Cut two Rack Sides (A) from 1×6 pine, each measuring 26 inches.

2. Using figure 1 as a guide, clamp both Rack Sides (A) together and cut a quarter-circle from the ends of the Rack Sides (A).

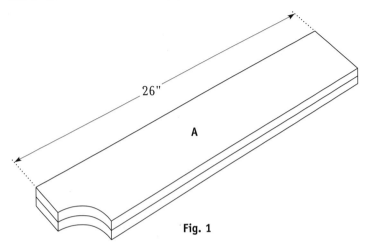

Fig. 1

3. Using figure 2 as a guide, mark the positions for the dowel rod holes. Using a ⅜-inch-diameter drill bit, drill into the marked spots ⅜ inch deep. (This can be done by placing a piece of masking tape around the bit ⅜ inch from the tip.)

4. Cut two Rack Top/Bottoms (B) from 1×6 pine, each measuring 24½ inches.

5. Place the two Rack Sides (A) on edge on a level surface parallel to each other and 24½ inches apart. As shown in figure 3, place one Rack Top/Bottom (B) perpendicular between the Rack Sides (A) 4½ inches up from the cut ends of the Rack Sides (A). Place the remaining Top/Bottom (B) between the Rack Sides (A). Apply glue to the meeting surfaces, and screw through the face of the Rack Sides (A) into the ends of the Rack Top/Bottoms (B), using three 1⅝-inch screws on each side.

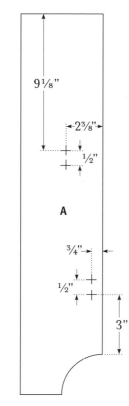

Fig. 2

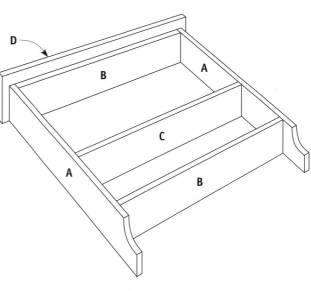

Fig. 4

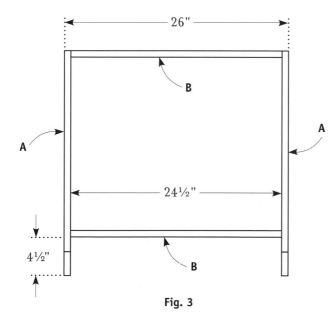

Fig. 3

6. Cut one Rack Middle (C) from 1×4 pine, measuring 24½ inches.

7. Place the Rack Middle (C) perpendicular between the Rack Sides (A) 13 inches above the cut ends of the Rack Sides (A), and screw in place.

8. Cut one Rack Ledge (D) from 1×8 pine, measuring 28 inches.

9. Place the Rack Ledge (D) over the ends of the Rack Sides (A) as shown in figure 4. Apply glue to the meeting surfaces. Screw through the face of the Rack Ledge (D) into the ends of the Rack Sides (A) using three 1⅝-inch screws on both ends.

10. Cut one Rack Base (E) from 1×4 pine, measuring 24½ inches.

11. Place the Rack Base (E) below the Rack Bottom (B) between the Rack Sides (A), as shown in figure 5 (page 104). Apply glue to the meeting surfaces. Screw through the face of the Rack Sides (A) into the end of the Rack Base (E);

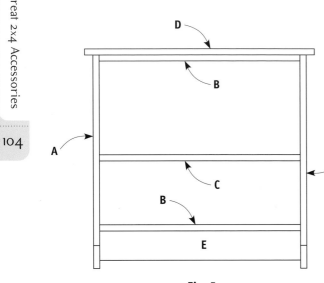

Fig. 5

also screw through the face of the Rack Bottom (B) into the edge of the Rack Base (E) using three 1⅝-inch screws on both sides.

ADDING THE DOWEL RODS

1. Cut four Dowels (F) from 3/8-inch-diameter dowel rod, each measuring 25 inches.

2. Wipe a small amount of glue in the holes drilled in the Rack Sides (A). Place one end of

the dowel rod into one Rack Side (A) and, slightly bending the rod, place the other end into the opposing hole on the other Rack Side (A).

FINISHING

1. Fill any cracks, crevices, or screw holes with wood filler.

2. Thoroughly sand all surfaces of the completed plate rack.

3. Seal and paint or stain the completed plate rack the color of your choice.

4. Attach the hooks to the Rack Base (E).

Birdcage

Here's a delightful fix for an uninteresting corner of the room. Although not designed for live birds, this birdcage is an attractive conversation piece with limitless decorative potential.

MATERIALS

3 linear feet of 1×6 pine

20 linear feet of 1×2 pine

18 linear feet of 1×1 pine

2 linear feet of 1×4 pine

2-×4-foot sheet of ¾" plywood

2-×4-foot sheet of ¼" plywood

HARDWARE

30 2½" (8d) finish nails

10 1½" (4d) finish nails

15 2" (6d) finish nails

4 small metal L-angles

2 small drawer pulls

2 2" hinges

150 linear feet of 18-gauge wire rod

Small spool of 28-gauge wire

SPECIAL TOOLS & TECHNIQUES

Dado

Router with round-over bit

CUTTING LIST

Code	Description	Qty.	Materials	Dimensions
A	Lower Sides	2	1×6 pine	11¼" long
B	Vertical Sides	4	1×2 pine	43" long
C	Upper Sides	2	1×2 pine	11¼" long
D	Back	1	¾" plywood	29"×13½"
E	Bottom	1	¾" plywood	13½"×12¾"
F	Vertical Front	2	1×1 pine	43" long
G	Upper Front	1	1×2 pine	12" long
H	Middle Front	1	1×1 pine	12" long
I	Lower Front	1	1×4 pine	12" long
J	Door Vertical	2	1×1 pine	25¾" long
K	Door Horizontal	2	1×1 pine	11¾" long
L	Tray Front	1	1×1 pine	11⅞" long
M	Tray	1	¼" plywood	11⅞"×13"
N	Top	1	¾" plywood	15¼"×17¼"

CONSTRUCTING THE SIDES

1. Cut two Lower Sides (A) from 1×6 pine, each measuring 11¼ inches.

2. Referring to figure 1, mark and cut out a semicircle on one 11¼-inch edge of each of the two Lower Sides (A). Our semicircle has a 6½-inch radius, but cut to any radius you choose.

3. Cut four Vertical Sides (B) from 1×2 pine, each measuring 43 inches.

4. Cut two Upper Sides (C) from 1×2 pine, each measuring 11¼ inches.

5. Place two Vertical Sides (B) on a level surface, parallel to each other and 11¼ inches apart.

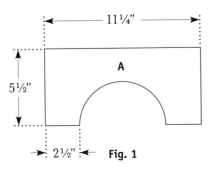

Fig. 1

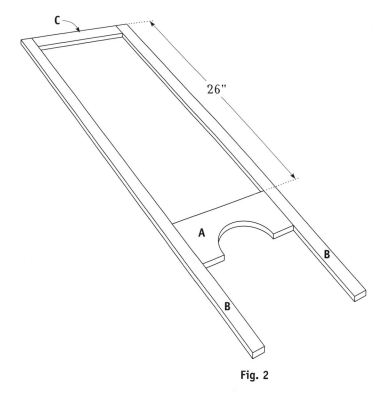

Fig. 2

Note: because of the relatively thin wood used for this project and the depth that the nail must penetrate, we strongly suggest that you predrill all nail holes to avoid splitting the wood. Place one Upper Side (C) between the ends of the two Vertical Sides (B), as shown in figure 2. Apply glue to the meeting surfaces, and nail through the Vertical Sides (B) into the ends of the Upper Side (C), using two 2½-inch nails on each joint.

6. Fit one Lower Side (A) between the same two Vertical Sides (B), 26 inches below the Upper Side (C), as shown in figure 2. Apply glue to the meeting surfaces, and nail though the Vertical Sides (B) into the ends of the Lower Side (A), using two 2½-inch nails on each joint.

7. Repeat steps 5 and 6 to construct another cage side using the remaining Lower Side (A), two Vertical Sides (B), and Upper Side (C).

ADDING THE BACK AND BOTTOM

1. Cut one Back (D) from ¾-inch plywood, measuring 29×13½ inches.

2. Place the Back (D) on a flat surface. Place one assembled side on edge, flush against one 29-inch edge of the Back (D), as shown in figure 3. Apply glue to the meeting surfaces, and nail through the Vertical Side (B) into the edge of the Back (D), using 1½-inch nails spaced about every 5 inches.

3. Repeat step 2 to attach the remaining side assembly to the opposite 29-inch edge of the Back (D).

4. Cut one Bottom (E) from ¾-inch-thick plywood, measuring 13½×12¾ inches.

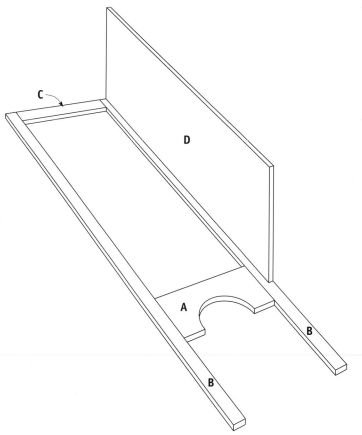

Fig. 3

5. Fit the Bottom (E) between the two cage sides, 29 inches below the top of the Back (D).

6. Apply glue to the meeting surfaces, and nail through the sides and back into the edges of the Bottom (E), using 2-inch nails spaced every 5 inches.

CONSTRUCTING THE FRONT

1. Cut two Vertical Fronts (F) from 1×1 pine, each measuring 43 inches.

2. Cut one Upper Front (G) from 1×2 pine, measuring 12 inches.

3. Place the two Vertical Fronts (F) on a flat surface, parallel to each other and 12 inches apart.

4. Fit the Upper Front (G) between the ends of the two Vertical Fronts (F), as shown in figure 4. Apply glue to the meeting surfaces, and nail through the Vertical Fronts (F) into the ends of the Upper Front (G), using two 2-inch nails on each joint.

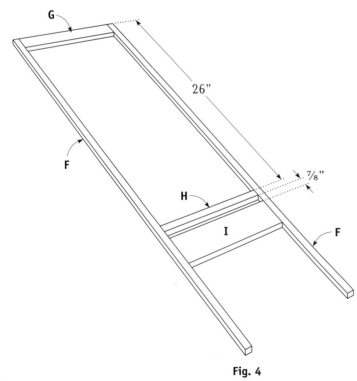

Fig. 4

5. Cut one Middle Front (H) from 1×1 pine, measuring 12 inches.

6. Fit the Middle Front (H) between the two Vertical Fronts (F), 26 inches below the Upper Front (G), as shown in figure 4. Apply glue to the meeting surfaces, and nail through the Vertical Fronts (F) into the ends of the Middle Front (H), using one 2-inch nail on each joint.

7. Cut one Lower Front (I) from 1×4 pine, measuring 12 inches.

8. Fit the Lower Front (I) between the two Vertical Fronts (F), ⅞ inch below the Middle Front (H). Apply glue to the meeting surfaces, and nail through the Vertical Fronts (F) into the ends of the Lower Front (I), using two 2-inch nails on each joint.

9. Fit the assembled front between the two assembled sides. Nail through the sides into the edges of the Vertical Fronts (F), using 1½-inch nails spaced about every 5 inches.

CONSTRUCTING THE DOOR

1. Cut two Door Verticals (J) from 1×1 pine, each measuring 25¾ inches.

2. Cut two Door Horizontals (K) from 1×1 pine, each measuring 11¾ inches.

3. Place the two Door Verticals (J) on a flat surface, parallel to each other and 11¾ inches apart. Fit one Door Horizontal (K) between the ends of the two Door Verticals (J), as shown in figure 5. Apply glue to the meeting surfaces, and nail through the Door Verticals (J) into the ends of the Door Horizontal (K), using one 2-inch nail on each joint.

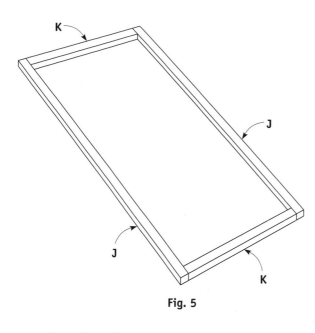

Fig. 5

4. Install small metal L-angles over each of the four joints between the Door Verticals (J) and the Door Horizontals (K).

MAKING THE TRAY

1. Cut one Tray Front (L) from 1×1 pine, measuring 11⅞ inches.

2. Cut a ¼-inch dado to a ¼-inch depth, centered widthwise, down the length of the Tray Front (L).

3. Cut one Tray (M) from ¼-inch plywood, measuring 11⅞×13 inches.

4. Apply glue to the meeting surfaces, and insert

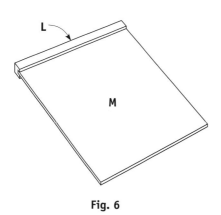

Fig. 6

one 11⅞-inch edge of the Tray (M) into the dado in the Tray Front (L), as shown in figure 6. Allow the glue to set up for 24 hours.

5. Install a small drawer pull on the center front of the assembled tray.

ADDING THE TOP

1. Cut one Top (N) from ¾-inch plywood, measuring 15¼×17¼ inches.

2. An optional step: use a router and round-over bit, and rout both 15¼-inch edges and one 17¼-inch edge of the Top (N).

3. Center the Top (N) over the assembly. It should be flush at the back, and overhang the sides and front. Apply glue to the meeting surfaces, and nail through the Top (M) into the edges of the Upper Fronts (G) and Upper Sides (C), using 1½-inch nails spaced every 5 inches.

INSTALLING THE DOOR

1. Attach two 2-inch hinges to the left side of the Door Vertical (J). Fit the door inside the opening at the front of the birdcage, and secure the hinges to the Front Verticals.

2. Install a small drawer pull on the right side of the door.

FINISHING

1. Fill any holes, cracks, or crevices with wood filler.

2. Thoroughly sand all areas of the completed birdcage.

3. Paint or stain the birdcage the color of your choice. We chose a pale yellow paint. After the paint dried, we applied a tropical wallpaper to the back of the birdcage, and random wallpaper cutouts to the front, sides, and top of the birdcage (photo, see right).

4. The bars of the cage are 18-gauge wire rods inserted into the Lower and Upper Sides (A and C). To install the rods, drill holes the diameter of the rods into the bottom of the Upper Sides (C), spacing the holes ½ inch apart. Drill corresponding holes (¼ inch deep and ½ inch apart) into the top of the Lower Sides (A).

5. Insert the end of one wire rod in the first upper hole, and cut the wire rod to length (¼ inch longer than the opening). Insert the cut end into the corresponding first hole in the top of the Lower Side (A).

6. Repeat steps 4 and 5 to add wire rods across the entire opening, fitting the rods into each of the remaining corresponding holes.

7. Repeat steps 4 and 5 to add wire rod bars to the opposite side of the birdcage.

8. Drill corresponding holes ¼ inch deep every ½ inch into the inside edges of the Door Horizontals (K). Insert 18-gauge wire rods into the corresponding holes, using the same method described in steps 4 and 5.

9. Wrap lengths of 28-gauge wire around each of the 18-gauge wire rods to hold the rods in position (see detail photo below).

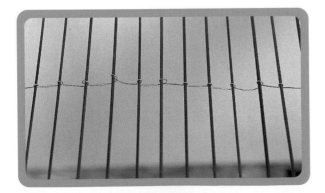

Display Box

This great accessory is both functional and decorative. The inside space is large enough for a variety of storage purposes, everything from keeping remote controls together to serving as a jewelry box. The piece is also useful for displaying keep-sakes, such as photos, treasured collections, or (as shown here) pretty shells.

MATERIALS

4-×4-foot sheet of ⅜" plywood

6 linear feet of 3¼"-wide crown molding

12"×11¼" piece of clear plastic sheeting, ⅛" thick

1 drawer pull

4 round curtain rod finials

HARDWARE

60 1" (2d) finish nails

4 1½" wood screws

SPECIAL TOOLS & TECHNIQUES

Miter

CUTTING LIST

Code	Description	Qty.	Materials	Dimensions
A	Lower Box Side	4	⅜" plywood	5"×14¾"
B	Lower Bottom	1	⅜" plywood	15⅛"×14¾"
C	Lid Side	4	⅜" plywood	2¼"×14¾"
D	Lid Top	1	⅜" plywood	14¾"×15⅛"
E	Long Top Trim	2	3¼"-wide crown molding	15⅛" long
F	Short Top Trim	2	3¼"-wide crown molding	14¾" long
G	Inside Trim	4	⅜" plywood	2"×11½"
H	Clear Sheeting	1	plastic	12"×11¼"

MAKING THE LOWER BOX

1. Cut four Lower Box Sides (A) from ⅜-inch plywood, each measuring 15⅛×14¾ inches.

2. Place two of the Lower Box Sides (A) on edge parallel to each other on a flat level surface and 14¾ inches apart. Place the remaining two Lower Box Sides (A) between the ends of the first two Lower Box Sides (A), as shown in figure 1. Apply glue to the meeting surfaces, and nail the sides together, using three 1-inch nails on each joint. Nail through the face of the overlapping Lower Box Sides (A) into the end of the Lower Box Sides (A).

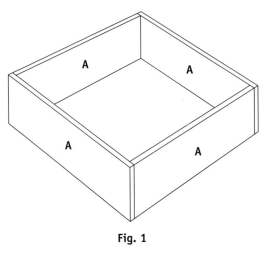

Fig. 1

3. Cut one Lower Bottom (B) from ⅜-inch plywood, measuring 5⅛×14¾ inches. Place the Lower Bottom (B) over the edges of assembled Lower Box Sides (A), as shown in figure 2. Apply glue to the meeting surfaces, and nail through the Lower Bottom (B) into the Lower Box Sides (A), using five 1-inch nails on each side.

MAKING THE UPPER LID

1. Cut four Lid Sides (C) from ⅜-inch plywood, each measuring 2¼×14¾ inches.

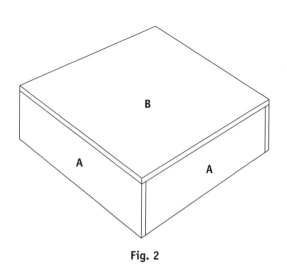

Fig. 2

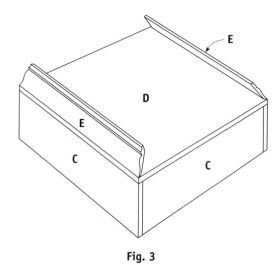

Fig. 3

2. Place two of the Lid Sides (C) on edge, parallel to each other on a flat level surface and 14¾ inches apart. Place the remaining two Lid Sides (C) between the ends of the first two Lid Sides (C), as for the Lower Box Sides (A) (see figure 1). Apply glue to the meeting surfaces, and attach the sides, using 1-inch nails. Nail through the face of the overlapping Lid Sides (C) into the ends of the Lid Sides (C).

3. Cut one Lid Top (D) from ⅜-inch plywood, measuring 14¾×15⅛ inches. Place the Lid Top (D) over the edges of assembled Lid Sides (C), as for the lower box pieces (see figure 2). Apply glue to the meeting surfaces, and nail through the Lid Top (D) into the Lid Sides (C), using four 1-inch nails on each side.

ATTACHING THE TOP MOLDING

1. Place the assembled lid on a flat surface, with the Lid Top (D) facing up.

2. Cut two Long Top Trims (E) from 3¼-inch crown molding at a compound 45° angle, each measuring 15⅛ inches. Attach the two Long Trims (E) on the long sides of the Lid Top (D), as shown in figure 3.

3. Cut two Short Top Trims (F) from 3¼-inch crown molding at a compound 45° angle, each measuring 14¾ inches. Attach the two Short Trims (F) on the shorter sides of the Lid Top (D), as shown in figure 4.

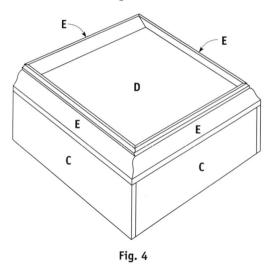

Fig. 4

4. Cut four Inside Trims (G) from ⅜-inch plywood, each measuring 2×11½ inches.

5. Place two of the Inside Trims (G) on edge, parallel to each other on a flat level surface and 11½ inches apart. Place the remaining Inside Trims (G) between the ends of the first two Inside Trims (G), as for the Lower Box Sides

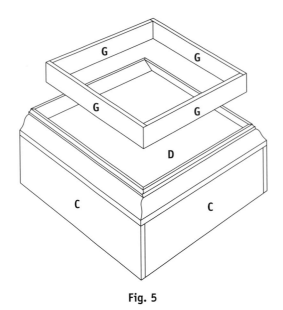

Fig. 5

(A) (see figure 1). Apply glue to the meeting surfaces, and nail the sides together, using two 1-inch nails. Nail through the face of the overlapping Inside Trims (G) into the end of the Inside Trims (G).

6. Place the assembled Inside Trims (G) inside the crown molding frame, as shown in figure 5. Apply glue to the meeting surfaces. (Glue will be all that is needed to hold the Inside Trims (G) in place.)

ADDING THE FEET AND THE PLASTIC TOP

1. Find the center of the 12-×11¼-inch piece of clear plastic sheeting (H). Use a ruler to draw two bisecting lines, each from opposing corners, as shown in figure 6. The center is the point at which the lines intersect. Drill a hole and attach the drawer pull. If you do not plan to change the decorative contents of the box, you can seal the plastic sheets with clear silicone.

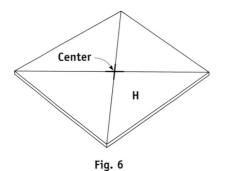

Fig. 6

2. Place the assembled lower box upside down on a flat surface so that the Lower Bottom (B) is facing up. Drill through all four corners of the Lower Bottom (B) in the locations shown in figure 7.

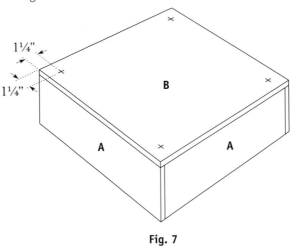

Fig. 7

3. To attach the curtain rod finials to the Lower Bottom (B), screw through the inside of the lower box into the curtain rod finials using 1½-inch screws.

FINISHING

1. Fill any nail holes, cracks, or imperfections with wood filler.

2. Sand all areas of the assembled display box.

3. Stain or paint your box the color of your choice. Here we've used a satin-finish maroon paint, and painted the feet white.

Folding Screen

Screens are wonderful accessories, and can block the afternoon sun, serve as a backdrop for a special table and chair, or even to divide a room in a crucial area. This pretty screen was first sponge-painted, then stamped with leaf motifs.

MATERIALS

2 4-×8-foot sheets of ¾" plywood

3-×4-foot piece of ¼" plywood

65 linear feet of ¾"-wide rope molding

HARDWARE

400 small wire brads

9 2½" brass hinges

SPECIAL TOOLS & TECHNIQUES

Miter

CUTTING LIST

Code	Description	Qty.	Materials	Dimensions
A	Main Panels	4	¾" plywood	16"×72"
B	Center Panel	16	¼" plywood	6¼"×9¾"
C	Vertical Molding	32	¾"-wide rope molding	13½" long
D	Horizontal Molding	32	¾"-wide rope molding	10" long

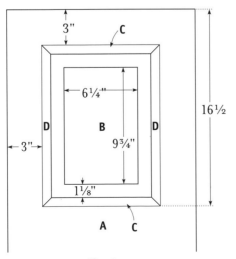

Fig. 1

CUTTING AND MARKING THE PANELS

1. Cut four Main Panels (A) from ¾-inch plywood, each measuring 16×72 inches. Fill the edges of each panel with wood filler, and sand the entire panel thoroughly.

2. Four smaller Center Panels (B) are attached to each of the Main Panels (A), then outlined with rope molding. The procedure is extremely simple, but requires exact measuring. For that reason, we suggest you carefully measure and mark each of the four Main Panels (A) with the position of both the Center Panel (B) and the Vertical and Horizontal Rope Molding (C and D). Begin at the top of one Main Panel (A) and, following the measurements in figure 1, draw the placement lines. Make certain that all of your lines are straight and squared.

3. Repeat the procedure outlined in step 2 three times to draw the placement lines for the remainder of the Main Panel (A). At this point, the Main Panel (A) should appear as shown in figure 2. You should end with 6 inches remaining at the bottom of the Main Panel (A).

4. Repeat steps 2 and 3 to mark the placement lines on each of the three remaining Main Panels (A).

ADDING THE CENTER PANELS

1. Cut 16 Center Panels (B) from ¼-inch plywood, each measuring 6¼×9¾ inches.

2. Thoroughly sand each of the 16 Center Panels (B).

3. Refer to the placement marks to attach one Center Panel (B) to the top of one Main Panel (A). Apply glue to the back of the center panel

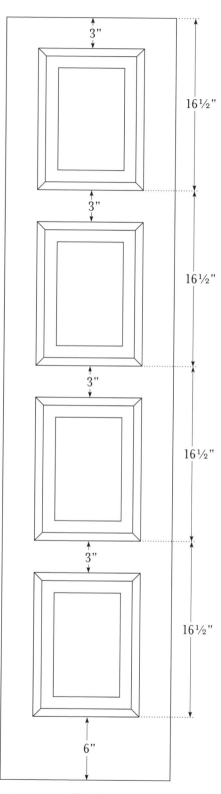

Fig. 2

(B), and attach to the Main Panel (A) with small wire brads nailed through each corner.

4. Using the marks as a guide, repeat step 3 three times to attach three additional Center Panels (B).

5. Repeat steps 3 and 4 three times, attaching the remaining Center Panels (B) to the three remaining Main Panels (A).

ADDING THE ROPE MOLDING

1. Cut 32 Vertical Moldings (C) from ¾-inch-wide rope molding, each measuring 13½ inches.

2. Miter each of the 32 Vertical Moldings (C) at opposing 45° angles, as shown in figure 3. Sand the cut edge lightly to remove any burrs.

3. Cut 32 Horizontal Moldings (D) from ¾-inch-wide rope molding, each measuring 10 inches.

4. Miter each of the 32 Horizontal Moldings (D) at opposing 45° angles, as shown in figure 3. Sand the cut edge lightly to remove any burrs.

5. Place one Main Panel (A) on a flat surface and position two Vertical and two Horizontal Moldings (C and D) to form a rectangle surrounding the first Center Panel (B), as shown in figure 1. Apply glue to the meeting surfaces, and use wire brads spaced about 3 inches apart to secure the Moldings (C and D) to the Main Panel (A).

6. Repeat step 5 eleven times to attach the remaining Moldings (C and D) to the remaining Center Panels (B).

Fig. 3

FINISHING

1. The options for finishing the screen are limitless. We first painted our screen off-white, and then sponge-painted over it with peach. We then glazed it with a mixture of half glazing medium and half peach paint. After the paint dried, we stamped each of the center panels with leaf stamps, using a pale-green latex paint. (Craft supply stores have hundreds of stamps to choose from.) See page 24 for more information on decorative painting.

2. The last task is to attach the hinges. Use three hinges between each of the Main Panels (A). You will need to alternate the hinges to allow the screen to fold properly. The hinge peg should face the back of the screen between the two middle panels, and face the front of the screen on the outer panels.

CD Cabinet

If your CD collection could use a little order, you need this terrific shelf. Placed on a table or desk, or hung on a wall, it will hold your CDs—and you may even have room for storing tapes and displaying pictures.

MATERIALS

19 linear feet of 1×6 pine

3 linear feet of 1×8 pine

4 linear feet of 3"-wide beaded molding

HARDWARE

50 2" (6d) finish nails

15 1¼" (3d) finish nails

SPECIAL TOOLS & TECHNIQUES

Miter

CUTTING LIST

Code	Description	Qty.	Materials	Dimensions
A	Shelf Sides	2	1×6 pine	34½" long
B	Shelves	6	1×6 pine	24" long
C	Shelf Top	1	1×8 pine	27" long
D	Base Front	1	3"-wide beaded molding	26⅝" long
E	Base Sides	2	3"-wide beaded molding	6" long

MAKING THE FRAME

1. Cut two Shelf Sides (A) from 1×6 pine, each measuring 34½ inches.

2. Cut six Shelves (B) from 1×6 pine, each measuring 24 inches.

3. Place the two Shelf Sides (A) on edge, parallel to each other, and 24 inches apart. Using figure 1 as a guide, place the Shelves (B) between the Shelf Sides (A). Position two of the Shelves (B) flush with the ends of the Shelf Sides (A), and the remaining four Shelves (B) inside the first two, spaced 6 inches apart. Apply glue to the meeting surfaces, and nail through the Shelf Sides (A) into the ends of the Shelves (B), using three 2-inch nails on each joint.

4. Cut one Shelf Top (C) from 1×8 pine measuring 27 inches.

5. Place the Shelf Top (C) over one end of the assembled Shelves (B) and Shelf Sides (A) as shown in figure 1. Apply glue to the meeting surfaces, and nail through the face of the Shelf Top (C) into the ends of the Shelf Sides (A), using three 2-inch nails on each joint.

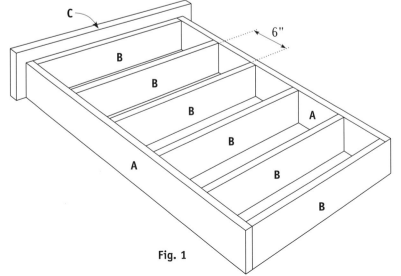

Fig. 1

3. Attach the Base Front (D) to the edge of the Bottom Shelf (B) as shown in figure 3. Apply glue to the meeting surfaces, and nail through the Base Front (D) into the edge of the Bottom shelf (B), using 1¼-inch nails spaced about 4 inches apart.

4. Place one Base Side (E) on both Shelf Sides (A) as shown in figure 3. Apply glue to the meeting surfaces, and nail through the Base Sides (E) into the Shelf Sides (A), using three 1¼-inch nails on each joint.

FINISHING

1. Fill any cracks, crevices, or nail holes with wood filler.

2. Thoroughly sand all surfaces of the completed cabinet.

3. Seal and paint or stain your completed cabinet the color of your choice. We chose a light cherry stain with a satin finish.

ADDING THE BASE

1. Cut one Base Front (D) from 3-inch-wide beaded molding, measuring 26⅝ inches. Using figure 2 as a guide, miter both ends of the molding at opposing 45° angles.

2. Cut two Base Sides (E) from 3-inch-wide beaded molding, each measuring 6 inches. Refer to figure 2 to miter one end of both Base Sides (E). **Note:** the mitered ends must oppose each other to fit correctly.

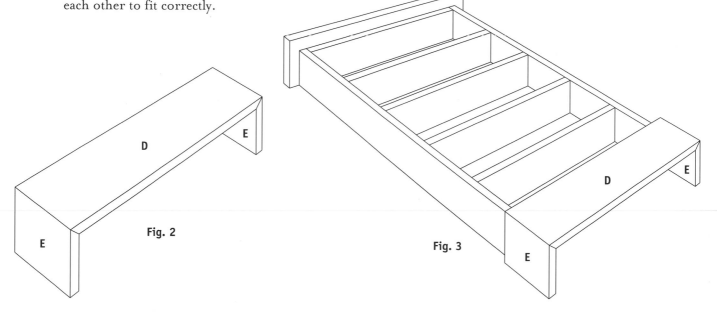

Fig. 2

Fig. 3

Desk Organizer

Too much work and not enough desk space? Make better use of your work surface with this handy organizer. There's room for scores of desk necessities, and the top surface is large enough to accommodate books and even a clock.

MATERIALS

12 linear feet of 1×12 pine

9 linear feet of 1×4 pine

6 linear feet of ¾"-wide cove molding

6 linear feet of 3¼"-wide crown molding

HARDWARE

50 1⅝" wood screws

20 1¼" wood screws

40 1" (2d) finish nails

SPECIAL TOOLS & TECHNIQUES

Miter

CUTTING LIST

Code	Description	Qty.	Materials	Dimensions
A	Vertical Dividers	4	1×12 pine	9" long
B	Shelves	2	1×12 pine	11⅝" long
C	Top/Bottom	2	1×12 pine	38" long
D	Front Trim	1	1×4 pine	40" long
E	Side Trim	2	1×4 pine	12¼" long
F	Back Trim	1	1x4 pine	35" long
G	Cove Molding		¾"×¾"	cut to fit
H	Crown Molding		3¼" wide	cut to fit

BUILDING THE CENTER COMPARTMENTS

1. Cut four Vertical Dividers (A) from 1×12 pine, each measuring 9 inches.

2. Cut two Shelves (B) from 1×12 pine, each measuring 11⅝ inches.

3. Place two Vertical Dividers (A) on edge on a flat surface, parallel to each other and 11⅝ inches apart. Center one Shelf (B) horizontally between the two Vertical Dividers (A), as shown in figure 1. Apply glue to the meeting surfaces, and screw through the Vertical Dividers (A) into the edges of the Shelf (B), using three 1⅝-inch screws.

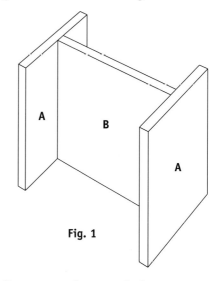

Fig. 1

4. Repeat step 3 to attach the remaining Shelf (B) to the remaining two Vertical Dividers (A).

ADDING THE TOP AND BOTTOM

1. Cut two Top/Bottoms (C) from 1×12 pine, each measuring 38 inches.

2. Place one Top/Bottom (C) on edge on a flat surface. Place one shelf assembly (A and B) 1½ inches from one end of the Top/Bottom (C), as shown in figure 2. Apply glue to the meeting surfaces, and screw through the Top/Bottom

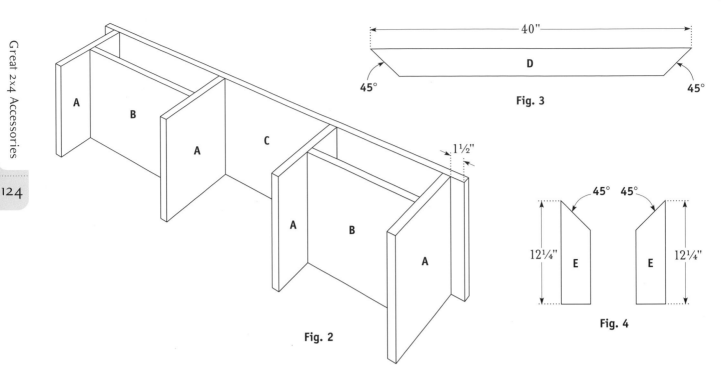

Fig. 3

Fig. 2

Fig. 4

(C) into the ends of the Vertical Dividers (A). Use three 1⅝-inch screws on each joint.

3. Repeat step 2 to attach the remaining shelf assembly (A and B) 1½ inches from the opposite end of the same Top/Bottom (C).

4. Center the remaining Top/Bottom (C) over the assembly. It should overhang the outermost Vertical Dividers (A) by 1½ inches on both ends. Apply glue to the meeting surfaces, and screw through the Top/Bottom (C) into each of the Vertical Dividers (A). Use three 1⅝-inch screws on each joint.

ADDING THE TRIM

1. Cut one Front Trim (D) from 1×4 pine, measuring 40 inches.

2. Miter each end of the Front Trim (D) at opposing 45° angles, as shown in figure 3.

3. Cut two Side Trims (E) from 1×4 pine, each measuring 12¼ inches.

4. Miter one end of each of the Side Trims (E) at a 45° angle, as shown in figure 4.

5. Place the Front Trim (D) over the edge of the Top/Bottom (C), as shown in figure 5. The Front Trim (D) should overhang the Top/Bottom (C) by 1 inch on the front and both sides. Apply glue to the meeting surfaces, and screw through the Front Trim (D) into the Top/Bottom (C), using 1⅝-inch screws spaced every 5 inches.

6. Place one Side Trim (E) over the ends of the Top/Bottom (C), with the miter toward the Front Trim (D), as shown in figure 5. The trims should overhang the sides by 1 inch. Apply glue to the meeting surfaces, and screw through the Side Trim (E) into the Top/ Bottom (C), using three 1¼-inch screws.

7. Repeat step 6 to attach the remaining Side Trim (E) to the opposite end of the Top/Bottom (C).

8. Cut one Back Trim (F) from 1×4 pine, measuring 35 inches.

9. Fit the Back Trim (F) between the two Side Trims (E), flush with the back edge of the Top/Bottom (C), as shown in figure 5. (This piece does not overhang.) Apply glue to the meeting surfaces, and screw through the Back Trim (F) into the Top/Bottom (C), using 1⅝-inch screws spaced every 5 inches.

Fig. 5

ADDING THE MOLDING

1. Turn the assembly so that the Front, Back, and Side Trims (D, E, and F) are against the work surface. Cut and fit ¾-inch Cove Molding (G) to cover the joints between the Top/Bottom (C) and the Front, Back, and Side Trims (D, E, and F). The molding should be cut at a 45° angle to fit the front corner, except the molding for the back of the organizer, which should be cut straight. Apply glue to the meeting surfaces, and nail through the Cove Molding (G) into the Top/Bottom (C), using 1-inch nails.

2. Cut and fit 3¼-inch Crown Molding (H) to fit around the remaining Top/Bottom (C), as shown in the photograph. Remember that the front corners are a compound 45° angle cut. Apply glue to the meeting surfaces, and nail through the Crown Molding (H) into the Top/Bottom (C), using 1-inch nails.

FINISHING

1. Fill any holes, cracks, or crevices with wood filler.

2. Thoroughly sand all areas of the completed organizer.

3. Paint or stain the organizer with the color of your choice. We chose a honey maple stain, then sealed it with a satin polyurethane.

ACKNOWLEDGMENTS

The authors would like to gratefully acknowledge the assistance of those who helped ensure the successful production of this book.

Many thanks to:

Laura Dover Doran (Lark Books, Asheville, NC), our editor, who accomplished miracles on an incredibly tight deadline, and who, on a personal basis, showed compassion and kindness.

Chris Bryant (Lark Books, Asheville, NC), art director for the photo shoot, whose talent, skill, and humor always get us through it.

Evan Bracken (Light Reflections, Hendersonville, NC), whose photographic genius is only exceeded by his patience and expertise.

Eric Stevens (Portland, Oregon), who created the illustrations and designed the book—thanks for your efficiency and skill under deadline pressure!

METRIC CONVERSION CHART

Inches	Centimeters	Inches	Centimeters
⅛	.5	12	31
¼	1	13	33.5
⅜	1.25	14	36
½	1.5	15	38.5
⅝	1.75	16	41
¾	2	17	44
⅞	2.25	18	46
1	2.5	19	49
1¼	3.5	20	51
1½	4	21	54
1¾	4.5	22	56.5
2	5	23	59
2½	6.5	24	62
3	8	25	64
3½	9	26	67
4	10	27	69
4½	11.5	28	72
5	13	29	74.5
5½	14	30	77
6	15	31	79.5
7	18	32	82
8	21	33	85
9	23	34	87
10	26	35	90
11	28	36	92.5

To convert inches to centimeters, multiply the number of inches by 2.5.

To convert feet to meters, divide the number of feet by 3.25.

SUBJECT INDEX

A

Adhesives, 13
Adjustable bevel, 16

B

Bar clamps, 19
Belt sander, 20
Bevel, 24
Board foot, 11
Brads, 14
Brushes, 13
Butt joints, 22

C

C clamps, 19
Chisels, 18
Circular saw, 17
Clamps, 18
Crosscut saw, 17
Crown molding (mitering), 23
Cutting tools, 16

D

Dado, 22
Decorating painting, 24
Dimension lumber, 9

E

Edge-to-edge joint, 22

F

Fasteners, 13
Finishes, 12
Finishing sander, 20

G

Glazing, 25

H

Hardwood, 9, 11

J

Jigsaw, 17

K

Kerf, 21
Knots (in wood), 11

L

Lumber, 9; buying, 9;
    common and select grades,
    10; cutting, 21; selecting, 10

M

Making wood joints, 21
Materials, 9
Measuring tools, 16
Metric conversion chart, 126
Miter, 23
Miter saw (power), 17

N

Nails, 13
Nails sets, 14

O

Orbital sander, 20

P

Paint, 12
Plane, 18
Plywood, 12

R

Rip saw, 17

S

Safety, 26
Sanding tools, 19
Saw blades, 17
Saws, 16
Screws, 15
Softwood, 9
Splits (in wood), 11
Sponge painting, 24
Spring clamps, 19
Squares, 16
Stain, 12
Stamping, 25

Straightedge, 16
Staple guns and staples, 15

T

Techniques, 21
Toenailing, 14
Tools, 16
Tools checklist, 20

W

Web clamps, 19
Wide steel tape rule, 16
Wood clamps, 18
Wood plugs, 15
Work surface, 16

PROJECT INDEX

Birdcage, 106
Birdhouse Floor Lamp, 78
Breakfast Tray, 82
CD Cabinet, 119
Cedar Keepsake Box, 58
Coatrack, 37
Coffee Table, 51
Desk Organizer, 122
Display Box, 110
Faux Poster Bed, 71
Folding Screen, 115
Footstool, 61
Grandmother Clock, 44
Kitchen Island Topper, 85
Ottoman, 32
Plate Rack, 101
Scrap-Wood Candlesticks, 97
Shell Mirror, 40
Wall Ledge, 55
Wall Table, 29
Wastebasket, 64
Wine Cabinet, 90
Wooden Window Valance, 68

RELATED TITLES FROM LARK BOOKS

Great Outdoor 2 x 4 Furniture: 21 Easy Projects to Build
By Stevie Henderson with Mark Baldwin
128 pages, color photos, b&w illustrations
ISBN 1-57990-036-4
ISBN 1-57990-047-X

Terrific 2 x 4 Furniture
By Stevie Henderson with Mark Baldwin
128 pages, 40 color photos, 120 b&w illustrations
ISBN 1-57990-066-6